# Living Prayer

# Living Prayer

*A Bible Study Calling for Action*

RICHARD L. BOWMAN

Foreword by
LEE A. MARTIN

RESOURCE *Publications* · Eugene, Oregon

LIVING PRAYER
A Bible Study Calling for Action

Resource Publications
An Imprint of Wipf and Stock Publishers
199 W. 8th Ave., Suite 3
Eugene, OR 97401

www.wipfandstock.com

PAPERBACK ISBN: 978-1-5326-9029-7
HARDCOVER ISBN: 978-1-5326-9030-3
EBOOK ISBN: 978-1-5326-9031-0

Manufactured in the U.S.A.                                    10/07/19

*This book is dedicated to my father, Leroy H. Bowman,*
*who continues to model what it means*
*to be in conversation with God*
*and to put that conversation into action in relating to others.*

# Contents

# Foreword

WITH THIS WORK RICHARD Bowman joins a great cloud of God followers who have been compelled by the Holy Spirit to not only seek God fervently in prayer, but to write books about that experience and discipline. One might ask, "Is one more book on prayer really needed?" My response regarding this book is a hearty "Yes!" It is both a testimony to Richard's intentional walk through life in conversation with God, and a unique encouragement to others to pursue a life of living prayer—unique because it is rooted deeply in the soil of Richard's own life experience.

As a young Christian I realized that for me (and I suspect for many others) the path to growth in Christ was not primarily found in the occasional special conference or large event, as meaningful as these can be. Rather, simple and regular spiritual disciplines of scripture study, prayer, and fellowship, accompanied by a life lived in daily service to Christ and others, is what has fostered steady Christian growth. Now, as a 60-year-old who has been on this journey with God as long as I can remember, *Living Prayer* has breathed new life into my walk with God and practice of prayer. Any relationship, including ours with God, can drift toward becoming routine and mundane without intentional nurturing. Working through this book has spurred me on in this most important of all relationships.

*Living Prayer* is founded on Jesus Christ, the living Word, and on scripture, the written Word. It is richly enhanced by the personal experiences of Richard and Elsie, long time disciples of Jesus. Their stories of walking and talking with God in faith and hope amidst life's challenges give it an integrity and authenticity that would be lacking in more life-detached, purely theoretical work.

Richard's writing is accessible to a wide range of readers. Even more, it helps to make prayer accessible to those who may think they don't know how to pray or don't possess the right vocabulary or technique to master the art of prayer. Understanding prayer to be about conversation in a relationship of love opens the prayer door to all.

To grow in understanding that prayer is not an activity relegated to just one of the many "boxes" in our segmented lives releases prayer to permeate and transform every part of life. To understand that prayer is more about growing a relationship than about a chore to do in order to get what we want makes prayer a joy rather than a job. *Living Prayer* will be a blessing to disciples of Jesus Christ and the world in which they walk as these truths are discovered and put into practice. I'm grateful to my brother in Christ, mentor, and friend, Richard Bowman, for responding to God's prompting to walk through life in conversation with God, and to share pieces of that conversation in the words that follow.

—Lee A. Martin, minister
SWAP, Mennonite Central Committee
Kimball, WV, USA

# Abbreviations

## BIBLE VERSIONS/TRANSLATIONS:

ISV = Holy Bible: International Standard Version®
NASB = New American Standard Bible
NIV = Holy Bible, New International Version [default, unless otherwise noted]
NRSV = New Revised Standard Version Bible

## OLD TESTAMENT BOOKS

| | | | | | |
|---|---|---|---|---|---|
| Gen | Judg | Neh | Song | Hos | Nah |
| Exod | Ruth | Esth | Isa | Joel | Hab |
| Lev | 1–2 Sam | Job | Jer | Amos | Zeph |
| Num | 1–2 Kgs | Ps (pl. Pss) | Lam | Obad | Hag |
| Deut | 1–2 Chr | Prov | Ezek | Jonah | Zech |
| Josh | Ezra | Eccl | Dan | Mic | Mal |

## NEW TESTAMENT BOOKS

| | | | | | |
|---|---|---|---|---|---|
| Matt | Acts | Eph | 1–2 Tim | Heb | 1–2–3 John |
| Mark | Rom | Phil | Titus | Jas | Jude |
| Luke | 1–2 Cor | Col | Phlm | 1–2 Pet | Rev |
| John | Gal | 1–2 Thess | | | |

# Introduction

"WHAT WE NEED IS more prayer." This is a comment I have heard many times in my years as a follower of Christ. To me such comments sound like judgement on those listening, but I have been assured by some that this is not the case. Usually it is a call for more public exercise of prayer. In the succeeding pages I will try to spell out what seems incorrect to me in this call for more public prayer.

Too often these words seem to imply that prayer is an activity we need to engage in so that God will give us what we seek. Do we really believe that God listens to us best if we pray more and harder? I hope not! God does not need to be convinced by many petitions to give us good things. How often have we heard this call or even given it ourselves? It has not been a rare happening for me, but I hope it will soon become rare.

This book will explore Jesus' example and teaching on prayer and the New Testament's record of prayer in order to understand more fully what it means to pray as Jesus wants us to pray.

What is prayer? Is it primarily a private or public exercise, or is it both?

Is prayer mainly a liturgical exercise or something we do to get what we want from God?

Can prayer be a way of life? Can we practice living prayer that is a conversation with God all day long? I believe this is what God calls us to do, to live! So, read on!

While this study can be used by an individual believer for their private study, even more can be learned and reinforced when the study is used in groups of two or three or larger groups, such as a Sunday School class or as a Bible study in a small group.

So, find another person or two to study with you, and pull up your favorite Bible on your computer or tablet or take it off the table by your recliner, then get out your journal or bring up your notetaking software. At least open your mental notebook and begin this journey. Each chapter is short enough to be easily read and digested, one a day or several in a weekend retreat.

Here is the game plan.

- Ask God for new and renewed insights.
- Read the designated Scripture section.
- Note any questions or comments that come to you.
- Read my reflections in this book.
- Follow through on any assignments, talking with God (praying) about the Scripture and its meaning as you journey through your day. It works best if this is begun immediately after reading each assignment.

In the following chapters, we will survey instances of prayer or praying in the New Testament along with passages where Jesus or the New Testament writers give teaching on living in prayer. While all printed Scriptures are from the *Holy Bible: New International Version*, please use whatever translation speaks to you the best. Since you will be wanting to see what each Scripture passage says to you, it is best to keep from using a paraphrased version since these Bibles tend to have one person's perspective on what the New Testament writers were trying to say especially when a passage may be unclear or have a variety of possible meanings.

Let's begin our study to see if prayer is simply a series of events, or if at its best it is truly a way of living.

---

*Confession.* I do not have it all together and do not even live totally as I want to or know I should. After 60 years of following Jesus, I am still on the journey to learn about and live more fully in a life of prayer. This gives at least one level of meaning to the artwork on the title page. It could also represent Jesus and me journeying together in living conversation (prayer).

# 1

## Prayer Is Living
## in Conversation with God

### READ: JOHN 11:34–44

[34] "Where have you laid him?" he [Jesus] asked.

"Come and see, Lord," they replied.

[35] Jesus wept.

[36] Then the Jews said, "See how he loved him!"

[37] But some of them said, "Could not he who opened the eyes of the blind man have kept this man from dying?"

[38] Jesus, once more deeply moved, came to the tomb. It was a cave with a stone laid across the entrance. [39] "Take away the stone," he said.

"But, Lord," said Martha, the sister of the dead man, "by this time there is a bad odor, for he has been there four days."

[40] Then Jesus said, "Did I not tell you that if you believe, you will see the glory of God?"

[41] So they took away the stone. Then Jesus looked up and said, "Father, I thank you that you have heard me. [42] I knew that you always hear me, but I said this for the benefit of the people standing here, that they may believe that you sent me."

43 When he had said this, Jesus called in a loud voice, "Lazarus, come out!" 44 The dead man came out, his hands and feet wrapped with strips of linen, and a cloth around his face.

Jesus said to them, "Take off the grave clothes and let him go."


## PONDER:

What thoughts and challenges do you hear and affirm in this Scripture?

What questions come to you as you read and pondered this Scripture?


## MORE REFLECTIONS:

While Jesus' prayer in verses forty-one and forty-two is our focus, we need the broader context to understand what Jesus was meaning by this prayer. A sentence or verse by itself can be very misleading, but one can never read too much of the surrounding context. Thus, in this book, Scripture for reading will always include more of the story than just the verses of our focus. This incident in John 11 is part of Jesus' interaction with Lazarus's sisters, Mary and Martha, after the death of Lazarus. To read the whole story, take a close look at all of John 11.

Now focus on Jesus' prayer (v. 41–42) in its context, and ask yourself or your study group: Why is Jesus praying out loud in public?

Might Jesus have prayed out loud to help the friends and family of Lazarus know that God has already been contacted about this situation? Jesus said, "Father, I thank you that you have heard me" (v. 41b). In addition to the NIV, many other English translations (including the NRSV and NASB) also use the present perfect form of the verb here, "have heard" or "have listened." This implies that Jesus and God the Father had been talking in the past about this situation.

By implication, Jesus is telling his audience that he lives a life of conversation both privately and continuously with God the Father. Based on this declaration, two millennia later we can also have faith that God always hears us as we live in conversation with him throughout our days.

This incident also lets us see that Jesus knew emotional turmoil. He wept as he went to the grave, and when he got there, "Jesus, once more deeply moved, came to the tomb" (v. 38). So, Jesus, as God who lived here on Earth as a person, knew sadness in the face of death. He also knew that persons might not fully understand his mission here on Earth nor have complete faith in him, so he prayed out loud while this was not his usual practice. The writer of the book of Hebrews puts it very well. He says that we have a high priest (Jesus) who knows our weaknesses and temptations (Heb 4:14–16 [ISV}):

> [14] Therefore, since we have a great high priest who has gone to heaven, Jesus the Son of God, let us live our lives consistent with our confession of faith. [15] For we do not have a high priest who is unable to sympathize with our weaknesses. Instead, we have one who in every respect has been tempted as we are, yet he never sinned. [16] So let us keep on coming boldly to the throne of grace, so that we may obtain mercy and find grace to help us in our time of need.

Jesus grieving at Lazarus's grave is an illustration of how he can fully understand us as humans. So, we may come to God without guilt or worry to seek his mercy and grace. God knows we are needy persons, and he is willing to have us walk in conversation with him, so we can avail ourselves of his mercy and grace. As Jesus would put it when he shared with his disciples the night before his crucifixion, "I will ask the Father to give you another Helper, to be with you always. He is the Spirit of truth, whom the world cannot receive, because it neither sees him nor recognizes him.

But you recognize him, because he lives with you and will be in you." (John 14:16–17 [ISV]).

The Holy Spirit is the spirit of Christ and the spirit of the Father, or to put it simply, the Holy Spirit is the Spirit of God. With God's Spirit with us and in us, we can live a life of conversing with God each minute of every day.

## TO DO:

Try this assignment for two days. Begin as you get up from your bed of rest by thanking God for the day ahead. From then on, whenever you think of something to praise God about, do it in a silent (or audible, if you want to and are not around people) voice. If you face a decision or situation that seems challenging, talk with God about it, too. He already knows about our lives, but it seems that we need to be able to talk with God about what we face. If this two-day assignment seems to add a dimension to your life that is good, then try keeping it as a discipline for your life's journey. I find it calming and restful just to trust this fully in God and his Spirit within me. Things do not always happen as I would wish (friends still die and stay deceased) but I am beginning to know the power of trusting God through Jesus and the Spirit.

# 2

# Prayer Is Addressing God

## READ: MATTHEW 6:9-13

[9] "This, then, is how you should pray:
"'Our Father in heaven,
hallowed be your name,
[10] your kingdom come,
your will be done,
on earth as it is in heaven.
[11] Give us today our daily bread.
[12] And forgive us our debts,
as we also have forgiven our debtors.
[13] And lead us not into temptation,
but deliver us from the evil one.'"

## PONDER:

What thoughts and challenges do you hear and affirm in this Scripture?

What questions come to you as you read and pondered this Scripture?

## MORE REFLECTIONS:

This is one of the best-known Bible passages even to those in Western countries who do not claim to be Christian. Thus, too often when we recite the "Lord's Prayer," we miss some critical concepts Jesus was trying to teach us. This might be because we say it from memory without thinking about it or because we repeat it as a spiritual talisman. The "Lord's Prayer" is not magic to be recited as a blessing on our activities. It will not help a high school football team win a tournament. It will not help political bodies to arrive at better decisions, unless it means we are all committed to God through Christ and his teachings.

If we read it carefully and thoughtfully as if hearing it for the first time as Jesus' original disciples did, we will notice that as his disciples today we have permission to directly address God. We can talk with the maker and mover of the Universe. We do not have to go to a temple to pray. We do not have to ask a priest to pray for us. And we do not have to sacrifice an animal or another human being for God to hear us. This is awesome indeed!

Just a month after Elsie and I were married in June 1970, we went to British Honduras (now Belize) in Central America where I pastored the Belize City Evangelical Mennonite Church. It was a very formative time for us as a couple and as individuals.

Belize, the Yucatan peninsula of Mexico, much of Guatemala, and a small part of Honduras form the region where the Maya people settled and developed their culture from 1800 BC to 1500 AD. They began and ended as an agricultural people. But, between 250 AD and 900 AD, they were also a flourishing urban culture. They built many stone cities and pyramidal temples. The Mayas also had a complex base-20 number system and a calendar using this numbering system.

During the urban period of this advanced civilization, human sacrifices were common, and they continued even into the early years of the Spanish invasions. Two of the common methods of death for the sacrificial persons were decapitation and heart removal. Scholars believe that many of the other local civilizations in Latin America during this time also practiced human sacrifice.

Now contrast this with the end of attempted human sacrifice in Hebrew culture when Abraham took Isaac up a mountain to sacrifice him because he believed that Yahweh (God) was demanding it. (Read Genesis 22:1–19.) To me this was Yahweh's way of taking a common practice in the Middle East during this time and showing Abraham that this is not the kind of worship God wants. Yahweh is God, and he requires perfect obedience. Since we are imperfect, finite humans, a sacrifice to cover our sins is required as a symbol of God's forgiveness. In the Old Testament this involved a regimentation of animal sacrifices, but in the New Testament, Jesus accomplished that requirement for all time and eternity. This forgiveness is for those who come to him as a son or daughter to a father—requesting forgiveness and expressing a willingness to obey him and accept his love. Jesus' life teaches us how to live, and his death, resurrection, and ascension are the necessary loving actions needed for our salvation.

One more aspect of addressing God needs consideration here. That is, how should we do it? Hopefully this is as we address our parents, siblings, and best friends. That is, we come with respect and trust. Rosalind Rinker in her book, *Prayer: Conversing with God* (Zondervan, 1959), shares an incident of a college student who prayed something like this, "Oh, God, thank you for life, oh, God. God, give us health, oh, God," ad infinitum. We should not use God's name as if it is an exclamation; we should use it as a personal name and do so with respect and faith that he hears us and can act on our behalf. (Rinker's book presented a watershed idea to me when I was in high school and college—how to pray to God as a group of believers in conversation. It is available at your favorite bookseller in paperback or as an e-book.)

With all of this as background, we can now revel in the fact that we can address God directly and even address him as Father. Some of us may not have had a good model upon which to base our understanding of Father God, but hopefully we have all had at least one person in our lives showing us parental love. This might have been a parent, an uncle or aunt, a grandparent, or a group home "mother" at an orphanage. Whatever the relationship, it seems to me that God will be fine if we replace "Father" in our hearts with whatever name we called the person showing us parental love as we grew up, e.g., "Nana God."

## TO DO:

Thank God that you can address him directly and call him "Father." Also, thank him for providing a way that we can become his children without the continuing sacrifice of other human life. Then thank him for bringing persons into your life who showed you what human love can be like as a finite model for God's love.

# 3

## Prayer Is Sharing with God the Needs of Others

### READ: LUKE 11:2–4

[2] He said to them, "When you pray, say:
"'Father,
hallowed be your name,
your kingdom come.
[3] Give us each day our daily bread.
[4] Forgive us our sins,
for we also forgive everyone who sins against us.
And lead us not into temptation.[j]'"

### PONDER:

What thoughts and challenges do you hear and affirm in this Scripture?

What questions come to you as you read and pondered this Scripture?

## MORE REFLECTIONS:

We are looking at the "Lord's Prayer" again, but this time it is as recorded by Luke. There is one more global idea that stands out to me and some other writers. The pronouns in the petitions of this prayer (v. 3–4) are plural ("we" and "us") and not singular ("I" and "me"). There is a place for our personal requests of God (in our closet, as the previous verses say in the KJV), but any public prayers should be universal praises and requests coming from the group. This can help us to move away from selfish prayers and to move toward caring about others who are our neighbors next door and around the world.

Studying some of the praise and worship songs that are popular in Christian circles today, we quickly find that these lyrics can be very selfish. I personally relate to some of the vim and vigor of these songs, but if I look more closely at the words I am singing, I often question what it is that I am truly saying.

One such example is the well-known chorus, "God is so good." There seems to be no consensus on the author and composer of this song. Some think the author was a persecuted African Christian while other say the first verse was written by a woman on a trip with additional persons adding more verses over the decades. Others claim that the writer and composer are unknown. Regardless of this uncertainty, let's examine the first verse.

> God is so good,
> God is so good,
> God is so good,
> He's so good to me!

Yes, God is good, and I want to praise him for this. He loves all of humanity with a tough love that sacrificed Jesus (part of himself) to save humans who trust in him for taking care of the consequences of their sins. But why do we water down this global statement and make it very self-centered by defining God's goodness as that which is aimed at us and for our benefit? Maybe we need to make it personal to make it real to us.

Before those who love the old hymns think they can get off with a free pass, let's look at the words to a classic hymn, "Amazing Grace," written by John Newton in 1779. Here are the first three verses.

> Amazing grace (how sweet the sound)
> that saved a wretch like me!
> I once was lost, but now am found,
> was blind, but now I see.

> 'Twas grace that taught my heart to fear,
> and grace my fears relieved;
> how precious did that grace appear
> the hour I first believed!

> Through many dangers, toils and snares
> I have already come:
> 'tis grace has brought me safe thus far,
> and grace will lead me home.

This is a powerful hymn that connects with the lives of many people—from those at the end of their ropes and trying to hide their hurts by regularly getting drunk to a royal couple at their wedding (Prince Harry and Meghan Markle). And it is very meaningful to me, personally. However, it is aimed very thoroughly at the one who is doing the singing or listening. It is not designed to reach out to others to invite them to experience God's grace. It does not make me want to help immigrants coming to the US border or those hurt in an earthquake and tsunami or the homeless person down the street.

In his prayer, Jesus was teaching us to pray for others and not selfishly for ourselves. I have quoted this prayer with others so many times in my life and have almost exclusively seen it as a prayer from me. So, what do I mean when I pray, "Give us each day our daily bread"? (v. 3). I do find that considering the "give us" to be a global request changes how I see what I own, the food I have, and the housing that I use.

Comparing this version of the Lord's prayer with the one found in Matthew shows us that they are very similar but not identical. Let's remember this the next time we are tempted to quote this prayer as a "magic bullet" to solve a tough problem in our lives. There is no magic in these words. This is a prayer extraordinaire because Jesus is reminding us that we can talk directly to God on behalf of all the needs—physical and emotional—of persons around the globe.

## TO DO:

Try an experiment. The next time you open a songbook or hymnal or sing from words projected on a screen or by memory, explore the pronouns to see how many of them are plural or singular. Also see how many of them are first person or second and third persons.

Then continue this experiment but this time explore you own prayers. How do the pronouns you and I use in our talking with God stack up with respect to how selfish these requests are or how much they are aimed toward good for others?

With these ideas in hand, try a new style of praying to God. For one week, be very careful in constructing your talking with God so that you do not only make requests for your own benefit but for the sake of others. I know this will be tough—been there, done that, and too often, still do it!

# 4

## Prayer Is Learning
## to Know Ourselves

### READ: LUKE 18:9–14

[9] To some who were confident of their own righteous-ness and looked down on everyone else, Jesus told this parable: [10] "Two men went up to the temple to pray, one a Pharisee and the other a tax collector. [11] The Pharisee stood by himself and prayed: 'God, I thank you that I am not like other people—robbers, evildoers, adulterers—or even like this tax collector. [12] I fast twice a week and give a tenth of all I get.'

[13] "But the tax collector stood at a distance. He would not even look up to heaven, but beat his breast and said, 'God, have mercy on me, a sinner.'

[14] "I tell you that this man, rather than the other, went home justified before God. For all those who ex-alt themselves will be humbled, and those who humble themselves will be exalted."

## PONDER:

What thoughts and challenges do you hear and affirm in this Scripture?

What questions come to you as you read and pondered this Scripture?

## MORE REFLECTIONS:

While Jesus is probably not showing his disciples how to pray by telling this parable, he is teaching us about the attitude we should have to keep our conversation with God alive and real. We need to examine ourselves with the Holy Spirit's discerning presence and then acknowledge what we find in our conversations with God. In addition to making praise part of our talking with God, we also need the reality of self-examination under the Spirit's guidance.

This self-evaluation under the direction of God's Spirit includes confession of sins and being aware of our need for mercy (forgiveness for what we have done or not done) and grace (to live as God's child even when we cannot do so on our own). Our reaction also involves checking out our inadequacies in bearing our crosses. And how are we doing on showing love and forgiveness to others? We begin with humility, honesty, and vulnerability as we explore ourselves and then extend these same values as we converse with God about those he has placed within our sphere of relationships. He already knows all about us, so we cannot assume we can keep anything from him about ourselves or how we relate to others.

The writer of 1 John reminds us that even as God's children, with our sinfulness covered through Christ's death, we still need forgiveness for our sins. "My little children, I'm writing these things to you so that you might not sin. Yet if anyone does sin, we have an advocate with the Father—Jesus, the Messiah, one who is righteous. It is he who is the atoning sacrifice for our sins, and not for ours only, but also for the whole world's" (1 John 2:1–2 [ISV]).

The tax collector in Jesus' parable in today's study knew he fell far short of satisfying God's criteria for his children, but he also knew where to go to find mercy, that is, to God himself. On the other hand, the Pharisee was sure that his behavior was perfect enough for God to call him one of his own. He "knew" that certain occupations or behaviors would not let one into God's presence. He also "knew" that fasting and tithing were behaviors that God required. He thought his actions were enough to make sure he was God's child, but Jesus let his disciples and us know otherwise.

Which person do we identify with in our praying—the humble tax collector or the proud Pharisee? Do we feel we have it all together by what we do and who we are? When we have honest self-examination, do we at times feel that we are part of a superior culture and ethnicity? Or in humble honesty, do we know that we cannot do enough to meet God on our own—that we need his mercy and grace? If we walk in continual conversation with God, we must admit that we do fail God and sin at different times throughout our days. So, in our conversations with God, we need to confess those failures and trust that God has forgiven us.

Also, as we walk with God through our days (in living prayer), we will quickly notice and be convicted when we do not "bear the cross" that God has left for us to carry.

> [23] Then he told all of them, "If anyone wants to come with me, he must deny himself, pick up his cross every day, and follow me continuously, [24] because whoever wants to save his life will lose it, but whoever loses his life for my sake will save it. [25] What profit will a person have if he gains the whole world, but destroys himself or is lost? [26] If anyone is ashamed of me and my words, the Son of Man will be ashamed of him when he comes in his glory and the glory of the Father and the holy angels. (Luke 9:23–26 [ISV]).

The "cross" here is metaphorical. Jesus knew that his mission would continue to the cross and beyond, so "cross" could mean our God-given mission. In any case it needs to be that which we put before all else for the sake of being God's children. Not all the gospel writers have the word "daily" with the word "cross," but Luke clearly wants us to know that any decision to follow Christ must be a daily lifetime journey. We cannot be a disciple only on Sundays and when we are with other Christians. We must always be Christ's disciples, and thus by implication we must always live in conversation with God. If we are not in conversation with God, we will for sure miss the twists and turns God has for us in our journey (our cross-bearing). Let's not miss the adventure in being God's children in his family.

## TO DO:

Today as you walk with God in conversation, observe those about you and listen for when the Spirit points out your pride and class-consciousness, then in repentance seek God's forgiveness. As appropriate, also ask forgiveness from those you judged or labelled? Do you find God exposing the prejudices in your life? Hopefully so. Therefore, ask God for forgiveness and for the Spirit's empowering to clear these prejudices from your life.

# 5

# Prayer Is Sharing Our Deepest Emotions with God

## READ: MATTHEW 26:36–46

[36] Then Jesus went with his disciples to a place called Gethsemane, and he said to them, "Sit here while I go over there and pray." [37] He took Peter and the two sons of Zebedee along with him, and he began to be sorrowful and troubled. [38] Then he said to them, "My soul is overwhelmed with sorrow to the point of death. Stay here and keep watch with me."

[39] Going a little farther, he fell with his face to the ground and prayed, "My Father, if it is possible, may this cup be taken from me. Yet not as I will, but as you will."

[40] Then he returned to his disciples and found them sleeping. "Couldn't you men keep watch with me for one hour?" he asked Peter. [41] "Watch and pray so that you will not fall into temptation. The spirit is willing, but the flesh is weak."

[42] He went away a second time and prayed, "My Father, if it is not possible for this cup to be taken away unless I drink it, may your will be done."

[43] When he came back, he again found them sleeping, because their eyes were heavy. [44] So he left them and

went away once more and prayed the third time, saying the same thing.

<sup>45</sup> Then he returned to the disciples and said to them, "Are you still sleeping and resting? Look, the hour has come, and the Son of Man is delivered into the hands of sinners. <sup>46</sup> Rise! Let us go! Here comes my betrayer!"

## PONDER:

What thoughts and challenges do you hear and affirm in this Scripture?

What questions come to you as you read and pondered this Scripture?

## MORE REFLECTIONS:

One of my most cherished incidents in the New Testament is this one where we eavesdrop on Jesus talking to God the Father. Jesus pours out his agony and despair over what he knows awaits him the next day—fake trials and death by crucifixion. And he knows that God the Father is aware of all of this. While I have not suffered such violence, I have had times of urgently pleading with God for a certain outcome while still being committed to following God regardless of what happens. In one such case Elsie and I were asking for a marriage to be saved. But after a critical weekend of intense prayer by several of us, the couple still separated.

Some Christian believers use this text as an example showing us that God will be moved by the amount of our praying for an issue (Jesus prayed for a long time and did it three times) and the depth of our pleading with him (Jesus agonized so much that "his sweat became like large drops of blood falling on the ground" [Luke 22:44 (ISV)]). However, to me, the depth of Jesus' emotions in this situation comes not from wanting to force God to see things his way but rather from his struggle to see things the Father's way and his struggle to be prepared for the day ahead and all it would bring. Luke explains, "Then an angel from heaven appeared to him and strengthened him" (22:43). I am glad that the physician Luke wrote one of the gospels because sometimes he replays parts of the story from the point of view of a person sensitive to what we now call biology and psychology.

Recently I was surprised by a deeper thought while doing some light reading in a "Christian" novel. Christian cozy mysteries and romances are often relaxing for me to read at the end of a day or when I am trying to unwind. (Now you all know my secret!) Michael, a character in *Nearly* (a book authored by Deborah Raney, 2016), finds that:

> In the dead quiet of his apartment the night after he left Claire's, he raised his fist and shouted at the ceiling. "I don't understand, God. I don't get it. Why are you doing this to me again? Haven't I suffered enough?"
>
> He ranted and wept. And then it came. Not an answer, certainly. Not an overwhelming peace. But in the silence after the tears and questions, a simple assurance. A knowledge that said, *I* [God] *have everything under control. It's not for you to try to understand. Only know that I am here. And I will never leave you.*

Raney, through her character, described the agony and the peace we can receive after telling it all to God through the Spirit within us.

Now let's examine this incident of deep and agonizing prayer by Jesus in the context of the surrounding events as they unfolded for Jesus during the week between Palm Sunday and Easter. Remember that Jesus had a successful day on Palm Sunday. Riding a donkey into Jerusalem was the sign of an overcoming king. The Jews, who had a long history of being overrun by the Babylonians and then the Assyrians, were looking for a political redeemer or Messiah (the Hebrew word for the Greek word, Christ). During the time period between the two Testaments, the Maccabean family had freed the Jewish nation from the Greeks (under Alexander the Great and his appointed leaders), but only a short time later the Roman armies conquered Palestine. So, the Jewish people were very ready to be a free nation again.

But Jesus, during what we might call "Easter week," kept confusing the Jews who expected a political Messiah. He forecast the destruction of the temple and the persecution of his disciples. For some this persecution would lead to their deaths (Matthew 24). Mark 14:3 (ISV) records, "While Jesus was in Bethany sitting at the table in the home of Simon the leper, a woman arrived with an alabaster jar of very expensive perfume made from pure nard. She broke open the jar and poured the perfume on his head." Jesus pronounced her act as a good one, preparing for his burial, while many others were flabbergasted at the waste of money.

The Jewish leaders questioned Jesus about with whose authority he did his miracles and preached his good news. He replied with a question of his own about whether John's baptism was from God or not. Since they were unwilling to declare themselves on the identity of John, Jesus did not answer their question (Matt 21:23–27).

Shortly after this, the leaders sent spies to test Jesus by asking a trick question about whether the Jews should pay taxes to the Roman emperor, Caesar, or not. Jesus answered by asking whose image was on a coin. "Caesar's," the crowd said. So, he replied, "Then give back to Caesar the things that are Caesar's, and to God the things that are God's" (Luke 20:25). Jesus' actions and teachings seemed confusing to everyone but Jesus.

It was a strenuous and stressful week for Jesus as he tried hard to explain his mission as the Son of God to both his disciples and some non-believing Jews. So, while we do not have much recorded of Jesus' deeply emotional conversations with God in the Garden of Gethsemane, it would seem like all the activities of the week and the days to follow would have been part of those prayers.

## TO DO:

Today begin to trust God's understanding by talking with him about anything that comes along and frustrates, frightens or discourages you. Pour out all these feelings, and let God carry them for you. He loves you and wants the best for you.

# 6

## Prayer Is Taking Time Away with God

### READ: LUKE 4:38–44

<sup>38</sup> Jesus left the synagogue and went to the home of Simon. Now Simon's mother-in-law was suffering from a high fever, and they asked Jesus to help her. <sup>39</sup> So he bent over her and rebuked the fever, and it left her. She got up at once and began to wait on them.

<sup>40</sup> At sunset, the people brought to Jesus all who had various kinds of sickness, and laying his hands on each one, he healed them. <sup>41</sup> Moreover, demons came out of many people, shouting, "You are the Son of God!" But he rebuked them and would not allow them to speak, because they knew he was the Messiah.

<sup>42</sup> At daybreak, Jesus went out to a solitary place. The people were looking for him and when they came to where he was, they tried to keep him from leaving them. <sup>43</sup> But he said, "I must proclaim the good news of the kingdom of God to the other towns also, because that is why I was sent." <sup>44</sup> And he kept on preaching in the synagogues of Judea.

## PONDER:

What thoughts and challenges do you hear and affirm in this Scripture?

What questions come to you as you read and pondered this Scripture?

## MORE REFLECTIONS:

We have already seen that having a life of prayer during the hustle and bustle of daily living was very important to Jesus. Now we see that he carved out special quiet times to talk with God the Father, too. In fact, a few such instances are recorded in the gospels. Here is one mention of Jesus' habit of taking some quiet time for pray and refurbishment, and in the next three chapters we will explore other instances of Jesus trying to take some quiet time to refresh his relationship with God the Father.

Here in Luke 4, Jesus had gone to worship in the synagogue since it was the Sabbath when he was in Capernaum in Galilee. There he healed a man in whom a demon lived. Later, he healed Peter's mother-in-law from a high fever. The people were so amazed, that after sunset (the Sabbath ended after sunset on Saturdays, so persons could be physically active again according to the Jewish custom) many sick persons were brought to Jesus for healing. By morning, Jesus needed a time away to refurbish his physical, emotional, and spiritual body.

Jesus was keenly aware of his mission. As recorded in Matt. 4:23 (ISV), "Then he went throughout Galilee, teaching in their synagogues, proclaiming the gospel of the kingdom, and healing every disease and every illness among the people." This is the same mission Jesus gave his disciples then and in every generation since then. Read the book of Acts to see how the early church carried out this wholistic ministry among the Jewish people and soon thereafter the non-Jewish people of the Roman world. Even reading the first few chapters can give a taste of this wonderfully composite way of living and sharing the good news of Jesus.

Also, in this passage from Luke 4 printed above, notice how Jesus got fully into his ministry of healing sicknesses and demon possession without it going to his head, so to speak. Jesus carried out rather miraculous healings, but he still did not want the whole community to know about it. Part of his thinking may have been so that he would not be overwhelmed by ministry load, but this also seems to be part of his humble following of the mission God gave him.

To express this healing power, Jesus had to be in close conversation with God the Father throughout each day. With all this happening in his daytime, Jesus also knew that he needed down time, time alone between him and God, in order to be energized for his mission the next day or week. Taking time away from the crowds was also a way to keep a healthy dependence upon his God-side.

When I get too absorbed in my God-given mission, I can often begin to put the emphasis on "my" in "my mission." We need to find ways to restock our Spirit-filled lives, so that we are reminded that the mission God is carrying out through us is "God's mission." If we place the emphasis on our activities, we become susceptible to Satan's temptations to pride and self-sufficiency. In the process we become ineffective in carrying out God's purposes. There are many examples of Christian leaders who lost their moral bearings and spiritual power because they became "important Christian leaders" and were no longer humble servant leaders.

The intimate relationship we can have with God through living prayer can become dried up if we neglect times of refurbishing and reenergizing our inner beings. We need to remember that our task is not to "save" the world. That is God's task, and he might use us in some small way to accomplish that goal. However, we might not even know when or how God is using us or which people's lives we are impacting. Remember the king's response to those he said would join him in his kingdom after the Judgement (as recorded in Matt. 25). Those on the king's right hand did not know when they had done anything for which they should be rewarded. The king said, "Truly I tell you, whatever you did for one of the least of these brothers and sisters of mine, you did for me." (v. 40)

After each of such moments away from the crowd, Jesus comes back to his mission of preaching and showing those whose lives he touched that the kingdom of God was near. For us the question will at times be: What is God's will for me in this situation? I know that when Elsie and I went to Belize instead of staying in the US, I had to struggle with which of these options God really had for us. But walking with God (in living prayer) and with others, particularly Elsie, I felt the affirming hand of God. May this be your situation, too, even if it comes after a lot of agonizing consideration.

## TO DO:

Do a self-care analysis to see how you are doing with making time to be busy in God's kingdom and time for rejuvenation (prayer and reflection) in a solitary place. As you go through your day, take inventory to ascertain that you are willing to help even the "least of these" among us and not just those who can help you climb the social ladder or who can help you make points with your boss or the chair of the committee you serve on at church.

# 7

## Prayer Is Sharing Our Agonies
## with God

### READ: MATTHEW 14:6-14

[6] On Herod's birthday the daughter of Herodias danced for the guests and pleased Herod so much [7] that he promised with an oath to give her whatever she asked. [8] Prompted by her mother, she said, "Give me here on a platter the head of John the Baptist." [9] The king was distressed, but because of his oaths and his dinner guests, he ordered that her request be granted [10] and had John beheaded in the prison. [11] His head was brought in on a platter and given to the girl, who carried it to her mother. [12] John's disciples came and took his body and buried it. Then they went and told Jesus.

[13] When Jesus heard what had happened, he withdrew by boat privately to a solitary place. Hearing of this, the crowds followed him on foot from the towns. [14] When Jesus landed and saw a large crowd, he had compassion on them and healed their sick.

## PONDER:

What thoughts and challenges do you hear and affirm in this Scripture?

What questions come to you as you read and pondered this Scripture?

## MORE REFLECTIONS:

This is another of several instances of Jesus trying to get away for private, renewing prayer and solitude. It begins clearly with Jesus needing some time to grieve over the unexpected killing of his cousin, John the Baptist, by beheading. But Jesus again finds that the need of the people around him is more important than his need to grieve.

While writing these chapters, a young child in our community ended up in the hospital on life support due to septic shock. As my wife, Elsie, and I struggled with the possibility of one so young dying, the topics of this book took on renewed meaning and intensity. How were we to pray? How could we "shake the gates of heaven" while still trusting that God's control of events would be good however things went? What did it mean to be living prayer in such a circumstance?

We pondered how to grieve if the child died. Now, several days later, we begin to hope that life would win, and this child would again be at home and in school. At best it will be a long journey. At worst, this life could still be very short. So, in a small way, I begin to feel what Jesus might have felt after hearing that his cousin, John the Baptist, had died. During such times, our spirits cry out for solitude—to get away, to lament, to cry, to shout in frustration, and to finally collapse in submission. This is what Jesus was seeking when he took a boat to an isolated spot along the lake, but instead he found a crowd with many needs who had followed him on foot. So, in compassion he got busy reaching out and healing the sick. May the Spirit lead us to discern when God calls us to persevere despite our exhaustion and to receive God's gift of enough energy and enough wisdom.

While the gospel writers record several instances of Jesus taking some time away from the crowds that followed him in order to pray, is this the usual way God wants us to pray? Apparently, our church culture and history lead us to that conclusion. Many of us try to be "good" Christians and have a period of Bible reading and prayer every morning. We call this our "quiet time."

There are many book authors and web writers who tout the idea of "daily devotions" for mature Christians. These authors include Billy Graham, Joni Eareckson Tada, John Piper, Marlene Kropf, the Revised Common Lectionary committee, and many more. Search with Google using "the importance of personal devotions" or "daily devotions resources" to find more specific web sites. Living prayer and studying God's Word are both important aspects of Jesus' disciples' lives.

However, we need to acknowledge that nowhere in the New Testament is it suggested we have such daily devotions. We have seen that Jesus took time away from the crowds when that was possible, so we know it has value for his disciples, too. And there are many Old Testament passages advocating the study of God's written (and memorized) word, e.g. Psalm 119. Verse 18 from that psalm says it this way, "Open my eyes so that I will observe amazing things from your instruction." Remember that the Old Testament was the only Scripture known to the early Christians. The New Testament letters and gospels were being written during the first century that the church was in formation. Thus, such Psalms would have given guidance to the early Christians.

To me, the worst application of this idea of having daily prayer and Bible readying in the morning is exposed when it gets interrupted by other, often unexpected, events of life. Often, we then feel that our world is off kilter for the day. But that is not how Jesus took such "interruptions." He saw them as part of his mission; these unexpected demands were expected.

Here are a few illustrations of the type of things I have heard; details are fictionalized. A young father reports, "Baby Marcus was awake all-night. OK, at least every hour from midnight until 5 o'clock. When I thought I could have my devotions, I fell asleep for another hour. My day at the shop has just been horrible." A great grandmother reports, "Since I am retired, I have been able to have my quiet time every morning. But I overslept this morning and was late to chair the Golden Oldies breakfast group. The meeting just did not go right."

Jesus clearly felt he needed some isolated time to talk with God, but he also clearly saw his mission was to preach the Good News (by deed and teaching) to all persons in this village and beyond. I am ashamed when I note that Jesus spent no time arguing for the rewards of solitude after a long mission but accepted what came into his life.

If we walk in daily conversation with God, we will want the grounding the study of his written Word gives us. So, while we are not required to read daily, we do need times of deep and meaningful study of God's Word. Making it regular is a good habit, but after living with guilt for many years because I did not read the Bible every day, I have accepted that I am not wired for that routine. As it turns out, I do study deeply when I prepare to preach, teach a Sunday School class, or write a book or article. These activities provide some spiritual disciplines for me. And I thank God for these times. Our days do not have to be defined by our guilt about "personal devotions."

If we are walking in living prayer with God, then we can tell him about all the ups and downs of our lives including any agony we must face. We will not understand it all in terms of human existence as defined by our culture, but we can trust that God know what he is doing in and with our lives.

## TO DO:

For the next week (or at least the next twelve hours), be aware of your emotional reactions. When you find yourself frustrated, angry, extremely low, or having to cope with death or separation, take the time to pull back to a place of solitude and tell it all to God. Then trust that God will ultimately make sense of it all.

If you have never tried a daily "quiet time" of prayer and Bible reading and study, give it a try. If your personality does not seem to fit this regimentation, try to spend at least an hour of such reflection time each week.

# 8

## Prayer Is Trusting God
## with Life's Storms

READ: MATTHEW 14:22–31

22 Immediately Jesus made the disciples get into the boat and go on ahead of him to the other side, while he dismissed the crowd. 23 After he had dismissed them, he went up on a mountainside by himself to pray. Later that night, he was there alone, 24 and the boat was already a considerable distance from land, buffeted by the waves because the wind was against it.

25 Shortly before dawn Jesus went out to them, walking on the lake. 26 When the disciples saw him walking on the lake, they were terrified. "It's a ghost," they said, and cried out in fear.

27 But Jesus immediately said to them: "Take courage! It is I. Don't be afraid."

28 "Lord, if it's you," Peter replied, "tell me to come to you on the water."

29 "Come," he said.

Then Peter got down out of the boat, walked on the water and came toward Jesus. 30 But when he saw the wind, he was afraid and, beginning to sink, cried out, "Lord, save me!"

[31] Immediately Jesus reached out his hand and caught him. "You of little faith," he said, "why did you doubt?"

## PONDER:

What thoughts and challenges do you hear and affirm in this Scripture?

What questions come to you as you read and pondered this Scripture?

## MORE REFLECTIONS:

Here is the third of four instances we are exploring of Jesus trying to get away for private, renewing prayer and solitude. This passage comes only seven verses after the text we explored in the last chapter. Matthew records that Jesus was healing and teaching until it was evening. The place they had ended up at was solitary with no immediate village nearby. So, what were the disciples going to do to feed the more than 5,000 people who had gathered to be healed and to hear Jesus teach?

As you may well remember or can read yourself, the disciples found a boy with five bread loaves and two fish. Jesus took these and prayed over them. This small amount of food ended up feeding 5,000 men plus children and women with twelve baskets of food left over. Jesus then sent the crowd back to their homes with full stomachs. This is where the verses we are studying begin.

In the previous chapter we looked at how we can talk with God about the agonies of life such as the death of a friend or a possible death of a young child. Here we are concerned with how to talk with God about the storms of life. Sometimes they might be real physical storms on a lake like the one the disciples experienced. But there are many other types of storms of life, too. For example, how does one handle the situation when young adult children come home because they have been expelled from college? Or how does a couple handle hearing about a shed on their property burning down while they are in mission service in Albania? (This last one is one Elsie and I faced a few years ago.) Or how does a person handle the pain of life when their spouse has been relocated to a memory care unit in a long-term care facility?

Jesus was heading away to put some of his own teaching about solitary time with God the Father into practice. He sent his disciples across the Sea of Galilee while he sent the now fully fed crowd home. Then Jesus went up the mountain to spend the night alone with his Father, God, in conversation. At some point in the night he looks out over the sea and sees that the boat filled with his disciples was having trouble with a storm. He does not hurry off to help them, but toward morning he does show up walking on the water near the boat.

What comes after the end of the printed passage is that impetuous Peter "dares" this spirit or person to truly identify themselves by a miracle. If it was Jesus, Peter wanted Jesus to call him, so Peter could walk on the water, too. Jesus told Peter to come, and he did walk on the water until he looked away from Jesus and at the stormy lake all about them. After that he began to sink until Jesus reaches out his hand and saves Peter.

So, what does this have to do with prayer; it looks more like Jesus is trying to teach about faith in God? As we noted in earlier chapters, this is just another indication that Jesus knew he needed time alone with God, the Father, and we do, too.

Secondly, note that Jesus was able to keep tabs on the disciples and their boat ride even though he was in an intimate conversation with God, the Father. Having a relationship with God through the Spirit and Jesus does not mean that we are going to focus primarily on prayer. In fact, if anything, Jesus focused on teaching and preaching to others along with conversing with God in prayer.

As we received word today of the death of the young child in our community who was on life-support, we were and still are keenly aware of this death and how it could potentially affect this child's family. As we walk and talk with God about this death, we deeply know the pain it brings to all who were and are in touch with the family.

Serving and caring for those in need and in pain is entwined with our conversation with God on a minute-by-minute basis about those in need and other situations we are facing. While we may not be fully capable of multi-tasking, God is! I am thankful that God does not have to take time away from other persons so we can talk together. In fact, one person's needs and answers to those needs may well be mingled with another person's resources. The global church is a large community of God's children, and we are called to share our resources with each other and the world around us.

My third take-away is that God wants us to personally work through our storms while having absolute trust in his control of the events of our lives. Jesus did not immediately go out and rescue the disciples in their battle with the lake storm. During our storms of life, can we recognize (as we talk with God) when God is telling us to hang in there and to not be afraid because God is present with us in the middle of every storm?

Lastly, this incident reminds me that we can and should share all our fears with God's Spirit while expecting great things from God. As we do that, we will find a faith that leads us to do things and brave events that we never thought possible. Also, when we fail to trust God as fully as we could, God will be there to recue us as we call out in fear while sinking in the morass of our failures. As we walk in living prayer with God, we can trust that the Spirit of God will pick us up when we fall and empower us when we falter.

In summary, let's take courage as we follow the advice given by the author of 1 Peter 1: 17–19 (ISV):

> [17] If you call "Father" the one who judges everyone impartially according to what they have done, you must live in reverent fear as long as you are strangers in a strange land. [18] For you know that it was not with perishable things like silver or gold that you have been ransomed from the worthless way of life handed down to you by your ancestors, [19] but with the precious blood of the Messiah, like that of a lamb without blemish or defect.

So, while we live in reverent fear of God the Father here in this land where we are strangers, we walk with faith that we have been ransomed by the death of Jesus, the Messiah. We have not been and cannot be ransomed by our own good acts.

## TO DO:

Today as you live in prayer with God, remember that God is there to walk with us through the storms of life. That means we always work under God's will and miraculous providence even in stormy and bewildering times.

# 9

## Prayer Is Flowing
## with God's Agenda

### READ: LUKE 5:12–16

[12] While Jesus was in one of the towns, a man came along who was covered with leprosy. When he saw Jesus, he fell with his face to the ground and begged him, "Lord, if you are willing, you can make me clean."

[13] Jesus reached out his hand and touched the man. "I am willing," he said. "Be clean!" And immediately the leprosy left him.

[14] Then Jesus ordered him, "Don't tell anyone, but go, show yourself to the priest and offer the sacrifices that Moses commanded for your cleansing, as a testimony to them."

[15] Yet the news about him spread all the more, so that crowds of people came to hear him and to be healed of their sicknesses. [16] But Jesus often withdrew to lonely places and prayed.

## PONDER:

What thoughts and challenges do you hear and affirm in this Scripture?

What questions come to you as you read and pondered this Scripture?

## MORE REFLECTIONS:

This is the fourth passage we are studying that refers to Jesus going away to a deserted place to pray. Four times the Gospel writers refer to Jesus going away to pray at a "solitary place" (Matt 14:13; Mark 1:35; Mark 6:32; and Luke 4:42), one time at a "lonely place" (Luke 5:16) and three times on a "mountainside" (Matt 14:23; Mark 6:46; and Luke 6:12). When you look any of these up to read, please read the whole surrounding context to see why Jesus went away and what he did there. In some of these references only Jesus is going to pray while others note that some of Jesus followers joined him.

There are two other situations we should note. One is Jesus praying in the garden before his crucifixion (Matt 26:36). We explored this occurrence in chapter five. The other situation is Jesus and a few disciples going up into the mountain where God glorified Jesus in a special way. We refer to this as Jesus' transfiguration. The three synoptic gospel writers record this event (Matt 17:1; Mark 9:2; and Luke 9:28). These verses begin the story in each gospel.

These may seem like only a few times that Jesus prayed in isolated places, but it was a habit for Jesus (probably not every day but often). As our scripture passage for today notes, "But Jesus often withdrew to lonely places and prayed" (v. 16). So, this time apart was a significant practice for Jesus, and therefore it should be a significant habit for us, too.

As I have pondered how times away with God have affected my life, I can think of two things. First, getting away from the rat-race of our modern world helps to give a deep and renewed sense of peace. Secondly, getting away from the busyness of my daily life tends to remind me that I am not the one in charge of my life.

Rather, God is the one who controls and directs life and its consequences when I surrender that control to him.

But it is also interesting to note that the Gospel writers refer to significant events of ministry in association with these times of withdrawal from the hustle and bustle of life. In the passage today, Jesus was confronted by a man with an obvious case of leprosy who begged Jesus to make him clean. Jesus reached out and touched the man and commanded him to be clean.

It is very significant that Jesus reached out and touched the man. The consensus among biblical scholars is that leprosy in the Old and New Testaments probably covered several different diseases as we know them today. The disease, commonly called leprosy in the past, at one time existed primarily in Africa and some Caribbean areas. It is now known as Hansen's disease and has been mostly removed from these areas. Regardless of which diseases it referred to in biblical times, persons being diagnosed with leprosy were to be ostracized by their communities until they were cured as declared by a priest. This included not being touched by other persons. So, Jesus reaching out and touching this leper was already part of the healing process. This act broke down cultural mores that separated lepers from others and their worship of God (Leviticus 13 & 14).

So, Jesus' priority was to care for the persons who met him and expressed their needs. In this case of a leper, he clearly acknowledged Jesus as "Lord" which indicated that he already believed in Jesus, at least at some level even if it was only as a person sent from God who could heal sicknesses. But I am also very glad that Jesus healed persons even when they had not yet formally accepted him as God's son. For one example recall the blind man whom Jesus healed as recorded in John 9. After Jesus smeared mud on the man's eyes and he washed in the Pool of Siloam, the man who could now see knew Jesus' name (Jesus was Greek for the Hebrew name, Joshua) but he did not know whether he was the Messiah or not. Some Pharisees were investigating this healing done on the Sabbath. "A second time they summoned the man who had been blind. 'Give glory to God by telling the truth,' they said. 'We know this man is a sinner.' He replied, 'Whether he is a sinner or not, I don't know. One thing I do know. I was blind but now I see!'" (John 9:24–25)

Only after Jesus had met the priorities of his ministry of sharing the coming kingdom of God with those in physical and spiritual need, did he then take time away with God. But remember that as we have explored earlier, Jesus was in continuous conversation (living prayer) with God his Father.

So, let's follow Jesus' example of proclaiming the good news that God's kingdom has come to Earth and is healing persons spiritually and physically. We will be resourced by God's Spirit moment by moment as we are in his service. And let's remember to avail ourselves of the times when we can get away to refurbish ourselves (physically and spiritually) in times of peace and quiet.

## TO DO:

Find some time to get away in the next day or two and spend the first part of that time connecting with God's Spirit. Just talk with him about the things presently on your mind. Then in the resulting quiet, ponder what such periods of quiet reflection do for you relationship with God. End with thanking God for bringing these benefits into your life.

Also, in the next day or two be aware enough to notice what ministry opportunities God is bringing into your journey in the kingdom of God. As you see these, ask God to help you know what you should be doing, and then do it.

# 10

# Prayer Is Admitting
# When We Get It Wrong

## READ: JOHN 11: 1–15

[1] Now a man named Lazarus was sick. He was from Bethany, the village of Mary and her sister Martha. [2] (This Mary, whose brother Lazarus now lay sick, was the same one who poured perfume on the Lord and wiped his feet with her hair.) [3] So the sisters sent word to Jesus, "Lord, the one you love is sick."

[4] When he heard this, Jesus said, "This sickness will not end in death. No, it is for God's glory so that God's Son may be glorified through it." [5] Now Jesus loved Martha and her sister and Lazarus. [6] So when he heard that Lazarus was sick, he stayed where he was two more days, [7] and then he said to his disciples, "Let us go back to Judea."

[8] "But Rabbi," they said, "a short while ago the Jews there tried to stone you, and yet you are going back?"

[9] Jesus answered, "Are there not twelve hours of daylight? Anyone who walks in the daytime will not stumble, for they see by this world's light. [10] It is when a person walks at night that they stumble, for they have no light."

<sup>11</sup> After he had said this, he went on to tell them, "Our friend Lazarus has fallen asleep; but I am going there to wake him up."
<sup>12</sup> His disciples replied, "Lord, if he sleeps, he will get better." <sup>13</sup> Jesus had been speaking of his death, but his disciples thought he meant natural sleep.
<sup>14</sup> So then he told them plainly, "Lazarus is dead, <sup>15</sup> and for your sake I am glad I was not there, so that you may believe. But let us go to him."

## PONDER:

What thoughts and challenges do you hear and affirm in this Scripture?

What questions come to you as you read and pondered this Scripture?

## MORE REFLECTIONS:

What shall we ask God for when we talk with him about a given situation? What should we discuss with God? Living prayer as a continuous conversation with God does not solve these questions completely. In this incident recorded in John 11, there are two groups of very confident persons who become very confused but, in the end, have a new depth of faith in God. We will study Jesus' disciples now and May and Martha in the next chapter.

Jesus' disciples were sure that the safety of Jesus was the most important item in the agendas for their lives at that time. Jesus and the disciples were on the other side of the Jordan River from Judea. In fact, they were in the region near the lower end of the Jordan River where John the Baptist had done his baptizing and teaching ministry (John 10:40). While John 3:23 seems to place some of John's ministry in the west bank area near the Jordan because there was sufficient water there, John 10 implies that where Jesus and his disciples were was on the east side of the Jordan and thus outside of the domain of Judean religious and political authorities. Note that John the Baptist was probably an iterant traveler in the whole desert area on the east of the Jordan River where Jewish groups such as the Essenes lived.

So, when Mary and Martha sent word that their brother Lazarus was sick, the disciples were sure Jesus would not leave his then current location of ministry and go to Bethany. At least that is what they argued for with Jesus (v. 8). Their conversation with Jesus (their living prayer) was pointing only one direction—toward keeping Jesus safe from the Jewish establishment. And they were sure they needed to let Jesus know what they thought.

When Jesus finally indicated he was going to Bethany to be with the three siblings, he shared his reasoning with the disciples. "Our friend Lazarus has fallen asleep; but I am going there to wake him up" (v. 11). This confused the disciples. When a sick person slept, that was a good sign pointing toward full recovery. Correct? But Jesus then openly tells them that Lazarus had died. This must have been even more confusing. They knew Jesus' power and history of miraculous healings, but now his friend Lazarus was dead. This was totally unexpected.

Are we quick to judge the disciples? Looking closer, I think I can imagine doing something like that. I know that God wants all people to be whole persons—physically, emotionally, and spiritually. So, of course I will pray for that with confidence. As I looked at a baby in Belize suffering with sickle-cell anemia, I prayed for healing and tried to find enough faith to believe it. However, that was not what happened. The baby died. I know that God did not make the baby sick, but for some reason he did not interfere in the natural sequence of this physical problem. I must trust that, as Jesus said in the case of Lazarus, "it is for God's glory" (v. 4).

At times it might seem as if we had been praying for the wrong thing given some of the outcomes we see even after we have prayed. But we need to trust that even when we don't understand what is happening or has happened, God is still aware of it all and is guiding us even in our times of living prayer. When we are close to a terrible situation (sickness, early death, fatal accidents, starvation, etc.), God does not ask us to discern what outcomes should show up, but the Spirit does want us to trust that God knows what is going on. We are not God! God is the one with the plans, the purposes, and the natural laws governing our actions, our lives.

Even when we are in living prayer with God moment by moment, we will still not get all our prayers "right." So, what should be the subject of our prayers? As Jesus told his disciples:

> [12] "What do you think? If a man owns a hundred sheep, and one of them wanders away, will he not leave the ninety-nine on the hills and go to look for the one that wandered off? [13] And if he finds it, truly I tell you, he is happier about that one sheep than about the ninety-nine that did not wander off. [14] In the same way your Father in heaven is not willing that any of these little ones should perish (Matthew 18:12–14).

We can always pray for a person to become a child of God and know forgiveness and the empowering presence of the Holy Spirit. We may for sure talk with God about these, even though we know that each person still has freewill to choose whether to come to God or not.

Another large topic we can always be in conversation with God about is what Jesus presented in his model prayer. He prayed to Father God, "Your kingdom come, your will be done, on earth as it is in heaven" (Matthew 6:10). Pray for justice, peace, and health to come from God's love being spread throughout the world, even when it looks like that will never happen.

This is enough for our exploration today. This topic of what to pray about will be pursued further in the next chapter.

## TO DO:

As you go through the events of your day, meeting people, and thinking about others, be in living prayer (conversation) with God about their relationship with God through Christ. This will change how we relate to them, sharing God's love as God loves us.

Remember that God loves each person just like a shepherd loves the one sheep out of one hundred who is lost.

# 11

## Prayer Is Getting in Touch with Our Faith in God

### READ: JOHN 11: 17-28

[17] On his arrival, Jesus found that Lazarus had already been in the tomb for four days. [18] Now Bethany was less than two miles from Jerusalem, [19] and many Jews had come to Martha and Mary to comfort them in the loss of their brother. [20] When Martha heard that Jesus was coming, she went out to meet him, but Mary stayed at home.

[21] "Lord," Martha said to Jesus, "if you had been here, my brother would not have died. [22] But I know that even now God will give you whatever you ask."

[23] Jesus said to her, "Your brother will rise again."

[24] Martha answered, "I know he will rise again in the resurrection at the last day."

[25] Jesus said to her, "I am the resurrection and the life. The one who believes in me will live, even though they die; [26] and whoever lives by believing in me will never die. Do you believe this?"

[27] "Yes, Lord," she replied, "I believe that you are the Messiah, the Son of God, who is to come into the world."

[28] After she had said this, she went back and called her sister Mary aside. "The Teacher is here," she said, "and is asking for you."

## PONDER:

What thoughts and challenges do you hear and affirm in this Scripture?

What questions come to you as you read and pondered this Scripture?

## MORE REFLECTIONS:

There are many reasons that our prayers are not answered as we were hoping they would be. But what went wrong in this situation? Did Martha not have enough faith? Or did she not pray hard enough? Or did she not understand what God's will was? While we need to acknowledge that Mary and Martha lived before the pouring out of the Holy Spirit on all believers in Christ, we can still presume that God knew what her wishes were. She obviously did not think her brother should have died. And it appears that she was mistaken, because in fact her brother did die.

Elsie and I were once part of a Sunday School class which another couple attended who was having serious problems with their marriage relationship. So, one weekend several of us bonded together to pray assertively for them to be able to work through some difficulties while they were at a guided retreat. They came home with renewed commitment to each other. But it was not long afterward until they were in a formal separation.

What went wrong in that situation? Those of us who were praying for the couple's marriage to be "fixed" were certain that this was God's ultimate will for this couple. So, did we not have enough persons praying around the clock for this situation? Or maybe we did not have faith enough. Clearly this was not God's will for this couple's marriage to break up. No, I believe all the above possibilities are wrong. God in his gift of freewill to humans honors the choices we make and does not remake them if we get them wrong. So, while God's wish would have been for this couple to not separate, he left them make that choice. (By the way, this was not an abusive relationship which would have been a sinful one to be sure.)

Returning to the incident we are exploring in John 11, Jesus, who was God and therefore knew more about the outcomes of our living than the disciples did, still wept when he was on the way to Lazarus's tomb (v. 34). So, I interpret this as meaning crying is a normal human emotional response when being confronted with the death of a loved one. Jesus' tears were also an acknowledgement that we wish the brother, sister, friend, or child would not have died. Jesus, although he is God, did not want Lazarus to die.

So, in addition to prayers for a person to become a child of God always being a legitimate subject of our conversation with God, prayers for healing and for life to be restored to another person are also good subjects to share with God in living prayer. The real issue is how we handle it when any of these types of prayer do not get answered as we wished. Can we in the middle of unanswered prayer still trust that God understands our concerns, frustrations, tears, and pain? Despite any of these, do we still trust that God loves us and controls our histories? Just as Jesus did in his conversations with Martha and Mary, he wants us to grow and extend our faith in him—our ultimate trust that he cares and wants the best for us.

My parents prayed for decades that a relative would come to know the forgiveness and security God can give us through a personal relationship with Jesus and the Holy Spirit. After a time of struggle, this relative came fully back to God the Redeemer. The example of my parents being in living prayer for someone for such a long time is a challenge to me since I had failed to persevere over this same time period. God's love can give persons opportunity upon opportunity to become children in God's family. This is God's will even while we have a free choice until we die.

Note that Jesus does not condemn Martha for wanting him to have come before Lazarus's death. She was sure that Jesus would have healed Lazarus, so he would not have died. Jesus does push Martha to consider her faith more deeply, and this is what he does for us, too. As we face life's storms, disappointments, sufferings, pains, and sadnesses, God uses such events to check our faith and trust. God does not make these events occur but does use them to help us grow.

While Jesus' male disciples seem to have misunderstood the meaning of his Messiahship, Martha got it right. Jesus had just asserted that he is the resurrection and the life, and she responds: "You are the Messiah" (v. 27). Martha's answer was clear and forceful. She knew that Jesus was not coming as a political ruler but truly as God our Savior.

Can we pray for wholeness for our friends, relatives, and strangers around the world (and for ourselves) believing in God's power and love while still in humility acknowledging that we are not God and do not know the outcomes of every situation. Sometimes it seems as if I never know God's will and other person's choices, but I trust that God through his Spirit walks with me in absolute love.

During our search for understanding God's power and love alongside of the bad things that happen in lives, let's not confuse God's knowing the outcomes ahead of time with the assumption that God has made these bad things to happen to us and others. In John 1:1–18, the gospel writer spells out that Jesus is the Word from God and all has been created through him. He goes on to say that if we have received him, we have become the children of God. This passage combines both the power and the love of God bound up in Jesus Christ. Peter, as recorded by Luke in Acts 2:23, used the words "God's deliberate plan and foreknowledge" to describe God's action leading to Jesus' crucifixion. Having a plan first makes foreknowledge redundant, so I see Peter putting God's plan first because that is a critical statement of faith about our lives. God is ultimately in control of our present, future and past; God has a plan for us. But all of this is because God has foreknowledge of the choices we will make. The writer of 1 Peter also puts these two ideas together, or shall we say they are in tension, when he wrote: "[We] have been chosen according to the foreknowledge of God" (1:2).

## TO DO:

As you journey through today and the next few days, notice when God through his foreknowledge took your mistakes and failures and weaves them into his plan for you which is a beautiful thing. Then thank God for this. The observation of God's actions and the beauty of our lives will affect how we face life. Let it put a wonderful calming effect on how you live.

# 12

## Prayer Is Trusting That God Knows Our Needs

### READ: LUKE 18:1-8 (NRSV)

[1] Then Jesus told them a parable about their need to pray always and not to lose heart. [2] He said, "In a certain city there was a judge who neither feared God nor had respect for people. [3] In that city there was a widow who kept coming to him and saying, 'Grant me justice against my opponent.' [4] For a while he refused; but later he said to himself, 'Though I have no fear of God and no respect for anyone, [5] yet because this widow keeps bothering me, I will grant her justice, so that she may not wear me out by continually coming.'" [6] And the Lord said, "Listen to what the unjust judge says. [7] And will not God grant justice to his chosen ones who cry to him day and night? Will he delay long in helping them? [8] I tell you, he will quickly grant justice to them. And yet, when the Son of Man comes, will he find faith on earth?"

## PONDER:

What thoughts and challenges do you hear and affirm in this Scripture?

What questions come to you as you read and pondered this Scripture?

## MORE REFLECTIONS:

Read the opening verse to this passage again. "Then Jesus told them a parable about their need to pray always and not to lose heart" (v. 1 [NRSV]). Wow! How could Jesus have been any clearer in sharing his affirmation of what this present book is about! And how could I have read this verse so many times over the past decades of my life and missed the significance of Jesus' direct statement of why he was telling this parable? As I confessed in the Introduction, I am still learning.

Maybe it would be good to see this verse in other translations. "Then Jesus told his disciples a parable to show them that they should always pray and not give up" (NIV). And here it is another version: "Now He was telling them a parable to show that at all times they ought to pray and not to lose heart . . . " (NASB). There is a bit of different wording but not in intent. They all show Jesus' direct meaning.

However, as compared to this direct statement of purpose, the parable is harder to understand. Jesus begins describing the involved judge as not caring what God or other people thought. I do wonder who put this judge into place and who kept him there. Surely, he cared about what they said. But that is not part of the story here.

This judge was badgered by a woman who wanted justice done over the person who was doing her harm. The judge was evil enough that the woman's pleas did not move him. The situation would probably have continued this way except that the woman's persistence finally became too annoying to the judge. So, he decided to give the woman what she was asking for—justice.

Now here is where Jesus made a giant leap, at least to me it seems that way. He now reminds the disciples (and by inference, us) that God has chosen us, "And will not God grant justice to his chosen ones who cry to him day and night? Will he delay long in helping them?" (v. 7 [NRSV]). So, what does it mean that we have been chosen by God? One thing this does not mean is that only a certain number of humans have been chosen by God to be his children. Rather, remember that Jesus began this parable saying that it was to convince his disciples to pray "always" (have a life living prayer at all times). He did not single out Judas Iscariot and tell him this was not for him. Jesus was still wishing for Judas to truly believe in him as the Messiah, the Christ.

So, stop reading here, and ponder what Jesus meant by calling his disciples persons who have been chosen by God. Then envision how the parable would need to be retold if God would be substituted in the story in place of the judge. Write your thoughts in your journal if you are keeping one for this study, or simply grab a piece of scrap paper and write your new story there.

---

OK, put down your pencils or pens. All right, I am not back teaching in the classroom. But I wish I was, so each of you could tell us how you would retell the parable with God, instead of the judge, playing the lead role. Here is my version.

> God in his absolute love hears us when we whisper, shout, cry or just talk with him in the midst of frightening experiences, when we mourn and don't understand why things have happened that have, and when we laugh joyfully in the rain and in the sunshine or as we wash dishes or the car. And when God hears us, he answers us giving what is best. Sometimes it is "Wait my child," "Come home my child," "Justice is counted only when all is complete," or "Jump for joy, my child."

(Feel free to email me your parables, if you so wish, using my email address given on page 114. I will try to respond but cannot guarantee it.)

To retell this story, whether we stated it explicitly in our heads or not, we had to decide which characteristics Jesus was pulling out about who God is. As opposed to the judge, I believe that God is just, kind, and caring. Or in short, God is love.

As to our behavior, what is this story telling us? It is not telling us that we need to pester God with our prayers until in disgust he gives us that for which we are praying. Jesus is also not telling us that God is reluctant to listen to us nor to give us good things. No, God loves us and dearly wants to show us his perfect love. As the gospel writer puts it in verse eight, " . . . he will see that they get justice, and quickly." In the cosmic scheme of events, God will move quickly. In our short time of existence, we sometimes feel that God is taking a long time.

When Jesus says we should "not give up" in our praying, does he mean we need to be persistent because God only responds to nagging? No, the point Jesus is making is completely opposite to the judge's behavior, so Jesus tells us to be in close relationship with God on a regular continuing basis. Our practice of living prayer should be routine. God does not see this as annoying behavior; God welcomes it!

Remember that if the Bible tells us what the meaning of a parable or story is, then we should not try to get it to say something else. With this parable, Jesus is not lauding the evil judge, rather he is encouraging his disciples, then and now, to be consistent in living prayer with God.

In summary, God will take care of his people because he is just and because he loves his own who "cry out to him day and night" (v. 7), i.e., they are living in prayer with God through the Spirit.

## TO DO:

As you go through your day, make a list of the characteristics of God you value. Then at the end of the day, thank God for expressing those characteristics as you see them in your life and in global situations while still giving us all freewill.

If you have not taken time to write down the retelling of this parable with God substituted for the judge, take time where you can ponder this undisturbed and "put it on paper," so to speak.

# 13

## Prayer Is Abiding in God

### READ: JOHN 15:1–8

[1] "I am the true vine, and my Father is the gardener. [2] He cuts off every branch in me that bears no fruit, while every branch that does bear fruit he prunes so that it will be even more fruitful. [3] You are already clean because of the word I have spoken to you. [4] Remain in me, as I also remain in you. No branch can bear fruit by itself; it must remain in the vine. Neither can you bear fruit unless you remain in me.

[5] "I am the vine; you are the branches. If you remain in me and I in you, you will bear much fruit; apart from me you can do nothing. [6] If you do not remain in me, you are like a branch that is thrown away and withers; such branches are picked up, thrown into the fire and burned. [7] If you remain in me and my words remain in you, ask whatever you wish, and it will be done for you. [8] This is to my Father's glory, that you bear much fruit, showing yourselves to be my disciples."

## PONDER:

What thoughts and challenges do you hear and affirm in this Scripture?

What questions come to you as you read and pondered this Scripture?

## MORE REFLECTIONS:

Living prayer may not be such a new idea after all. Here John recorded Jesus urging his disciples, "Remain in me, as I also remain in you" (v. 4). This kind of mutual "being in the other" seems strange since we cannot envision how this can be physically. I do not wonder why his disciples had a hard time understanding this and similar allusions that Jesus used. For one example, we can just go back to the beginning of this discourse. Just after Jesus washed the disciples' feet, he told Peter, "Where I am going, you cannot follow now, but you will follow later" (John 13:36). That was confusing for Peter, too.

This passage is part of Jesus' major farewell teachings (while in the upper room before his crucifixion) in what modern translations of the Bible label as John 13–17. At the end of this time of teaching the disciples and talking to God on their behalf, Jesus took his disciples across the Kidron Valley and into the Garden of Gethsemane. From there he would be arrested, tried, and crucified, followed by his resurrection from the dead and ascension back to the Father. So, Jesus knew he was not going to be with the disciples much longer.

Thus, Jesus comments about being one with his disciples must have referred to a spiritual association since he knew he would not be physically on the Earth much longer. As we remain in Jesus, seeking his forgiveness and grace, he is also in us in the person of the Holy Spirit, empowering us to live as his disciples. This is truly another way to describe "living prayer."

Let's look further at the meaning of our being in Jesus and he in us. Jesus uses the metaphor of a vine and its branches. So, in this example, the branches need to be attached to—connected to—and growing from the vine in order to be healthy branches that will bear fruit—grapes. On the cellular level, macroscopic plants, except for mosses and algae, use tubes (in vascular bundles) to transport water and nutrients to all sections of the plant. (While the people of Jesus' day did not know about cells and their role in living tissue, they did understand the basic general ideas of flow and connectedness explained in more detail below.)

Examples of vascular plants include grape vines, grain crops, and trees. These have vascular bundles composed of xylem (surrounded by phloem) in the form of tubes. Xylem transports water and dissolved minerals from the roots into the rest of the plant while phloem moves dissolved sugars. Sugar and oxygen molecules are formed from water and carbon dioxide during the process of photosynthesis which is then used for energy by a plant's cells. Plant cells need oxygen to metabolize sugar converting it into usable energy. Thus, at nighttime, the plant's cells get oxygen from the air outside of the leaves which is transported by the vascular bundles to all the other cells.

In woody plants, such as trees, the vascular bundles and other living and protective material are in the outer layers of branches and trunks. The inner material of these layers forms the woody section in the middle of the cross-section of these entities. This woody growth provides structural rigidity and flexibility for the branches and trunks.

If one or more vascular bundles are cut, the plant's cells on the side of the cut away from the roots will be damaged due to the lack of enough water and minerals. If all the vascular bundles are cut, then these cells will die. In fact, if a vascular bundle is cut, then oxygen cannot flow from the damaged leaves to the rest of the body.

So, if we ask which is more important, the stem, trunk (if present), and the roots of a plant or the branches and the leaves, we cannot form a straightforward answer. The plant needs all its parts being healthy for the whole plant to remain healthy and growing.

This is how it is with the concept of us being in Christ and his being in us. It is a complicated interaction and cannot be easily separated to be analyzed. But maybe we can see a bit how our spiritual lives fit this metaphor. Being in Jesus provides connectedness that supports us in our daily living and gives us directions for our lives. Jesus being in us gives us the living presence of the Holy Spirit of God, so we have the energy, wisdom, and commitment to grow as God wants. That is, the Spirit gives us the ability to grow and be what God wants us to be.

Just as healthy macroscopic plants produce fruit (seeds, with or without fruity flesh), our healthy spiritual lives will also produce fruit. In the case of Christian believers, this fruit will be doing what God wants us to do—loving others, obeying him, sharing with others the good news of salvation through Jesus Christ, working to bring peace to human endeavors, putting God and others ahead of our own desires, and similar behaviors. All of this will involve being in close relationship with Jesus every moment of every day.

Living prayer (being in conversation) with God is truly being in him and he in us. We will then bear fruit that will glorify God.

## TO DO:

Today, let being in living prayer with God mean taking time to evaluate how your relationship with God is going. Are you depending upon God to carry you through life's ups and downs (Jesus being in you)? Are you seeking God's wisdom and direction for the decisions and choices that comes your way today (being in Jesus)? Ask God for his forgiveness when going your own way gets ahead of being in Christ. And thank God for the peace and love you sense from the Spirit when you know you are in Christ. Revel in the security of Christ being in you and of you being in Christ.

# 14

## Prayer Is Daily Walking and Talking with Jesus

### READ: LUKE 24:13-16, 25-33A

¹³ Now that same day two of them were going to a village called Emmaus, about seven miles from Jerusalem. ¹⁴ They were talking with each other about everything that had happened. ¹⁵ As they talked and discussed these things with each other, Jesus himself came up and walked along with them; ¹⁶ but they were kept from recognizing him.

²⁵ He said to them, "How foolish you are, and how slow to believe all that the prophets have spoken! ²⁶ Did not the Messiah have to suffer these things and then enter his glory?" ²⁷ And beginning with Moses and all the Prophets, he explained to them what was said in all the Scriptures concerning himself.

²⁸ As they approached the village to which they were going, Jesus continued on as if he were going farther. ²⁹ But they urged him strongly, "Stay with us, for it is nearly evening; the day is almost over." So he went in to stay with them.

³⁰ When he was at the table with them, he took bread, gave thanks, broke it and began to give it to them.

<sup>31</sup> Then their eyes were opened and they recognized him, and he disappeared from their sight. <sup>32</sup> They asked each other, "Were not our hearts burning within us while he talked with us on the road and opened the Scriptures to us?"
<sup>33</sup> They got up and returned at once to Jerusalem.

## PONDER:

What thoughts and challenges do you hear and affirm in this Scripture?

What questions come to you as you read and pondered this Scripture?

## MORE REFLECTIONS:

In the last chapter we looked at Jesus teaching about how we are to abide in him and he in us. The passage for this chapter is an example of how Jesus' disciples can practice living prayer (conversation) with God even when we are confused and get it wrong at first. Most of the time I know it is God who I am talking with in living prayer, but I do not always see what God is doing with me, others, and our situations. In faith we walk through our lives trusting that God is doing a good thing in and through us even though it might look to be otherwise.

Now take time to reread the passage from Luke 23 above. This time make a written list (or a mental one, if you are not yet 70 and can do that!) of the positive characteristics of the two persons who walked to Emmaus that day. Stop now and make that list before moving on.

___

Here is the list of characteristics I came up with by studying the two persons walking to Emmaus and interacting with the risen Jesus. My goal is to emulate these in my own life, but too often I find I lack in doing this in many ways. However, energy can come from reaching for these as goals and from confessing to God and to others our failures, asking for forgiveness.

## Honesty.

These two persons readily shared their disappointments with Jesus as they walked along the road. And when they arrived back where the other believers were gathered in Jerusalem, they quickly owned up to the fact that they did not recognize Jesus until he broke the bread at their shared meal. They lived honesty.

## Vulnerability.

Being honest often means that we must open ourselves up to being misunderstood by others and, in the case of opening up to Jesus, being willing to accept the outcomes of our sharing even when God seems not to answer us nor to do what we asked. There have been several occasions in my life where I have sensed that, in my conversations with God, I was being told I needed to ask someone's forgiveness for my behavior. In one situation I am thinking of, I still thought the other person had behaved in a way that was not God-driven, but that was not for me to fix. I needed to heed God and address my behavior. Most times there was a re-establishment of enhanced relationships, so why did I balk at being open about my contributions to the breaks in relationships? Being vulnerable often seems very risky until we implement it in life.

## Teachability.

As we open ourselves to God, we do so to learn from him about how to be and how to live. We are called disciples because we want to learn from our teacher—we want to follow Jesus Christ through God's Spirit.

## Correctability.

This is a companion to teachability. If we are willing to learn new ways, we need also to be open to being corrected when we begin to go down the wrong way.

The author of Hebrews 12:5b–6 (NRSV) quotes Proverbs 3:11–12 (from the Septuagint):

> [5b] "My child, do not regard lightly the discipline of the Lord,
>     or lose heart when you are punished by him;
> [6] for the Lord disciplines those whom he loves,
>     and chastises every child whom he accepts."

To discipline and to chastise may not sound like comforting verbs when we are on the receiving end, but I sense that the writer of Hebrews and the author of Proverbs meant for us to be encouraged. To know and trust that God loves us even when we feel like some of the events of our lives are failures may not be pleasant, but it should be reassuring knowing God knows our lives and cares about how we live.

We are finite persons and not God, so we do not know everything (do not have absolute knowledge) nor do we perfectly follow God's directions for our lives. We need correction for both the mistakes and the sins we commit.

## Hospitality.

I grew up in a Pennsylvania German community in Pennsylvania where typically one assumed that the first invitation to stay for dinner or lunch was just a polite offering and that the visitor should answer, "no." However, after the invitation was repeated once or twice more, then one could humbly accept. So, I identify with the comment here that Jesus was ready to continue his journey when the two travelers "urged him strongly" to stay for the night. I read this as meaning that they probably gladly offered the invitation several times.

This is the kind of hospitality I want to practice, not the planned ahead with lots of time to prepare, but the spur-of-the-moment offering because the situation warrants it (God's Spirit is urging me to do this). This would be the caring for strangers, which Jesus lauds in Matthew 25 as he discusses the future judgement using the metaphor of a shepherd and sheep and goats.

## Generosity.

The companion to hospitality the travelers offered Jesus is their generosity to share what they had: food, a place to stay for the night, and fellowship. None of these may have been elaborate, but what they had, they offered. This is all God asks from us—to share what we have.

## Excited sharing of the good news.

These two believers had just walked the roughly seven miles (around 11 km) from Jerusalem to Emmaus. After we left them at the end of the Scripture above, they were doing the return journey just to share the exciting news that they had seen Jesus. One of my life goals is to live with this kind of eagerness to talk with others about my faith in God through Jesus. I also want to walk in living prayers with the Spirit so that I know when to talk and when to just be.

In summary, how wonderful it must have been after the two persons living in Emmaus had connected with Jesus on their journey home. I can imagine that they talked with Jesus about the meaning of all the events that had happened the week before the resurrection We participate in a similar relationship as we converse with God throughout our days in living prayer. And let us shout with the writer of Hebrews 12:1–2a:

> [1] Therefore, since we are surrounded by such a great cloud of witnesses, let us throw off everything that hinders and the sin that so easily entangles. And let us run

with perseverance the race marked out for us, [2] fixing our eyes on Jesus, the pioneer and perfecter of faith.

## TO DO:

Choose one of the characteristics explored in this chapter and specifically attempt to add or enhance this to your living in prayer relationship with God. And try adding it to your relationship with at least one other person, whether they are friends or strangers, in the next two days.B

# 15

## Prayer Is Agreeing
## with and Forgiving Others

### READ: MATTHEW 18:19–22

[19] "Again, truly I tell you that if two of you on earth agree about anything they ask for, it will be done for them by my Father in heaven. [20] For where two or three gather in my name, there am I with them."

[21] Then Peter came to Jesus and asked, "Lord, how many times shall I forgive my brother or sister who sins against me? Up to seven times?"

[22] Jesus answered, "I tell you, not seven times, but seventy-seven times.

### PONDER:

What thoughts and challenges do you hear and affirm in this Scripture?

What questions come to you as you read and pondered this Scripture?

## MORE REFLECTIONS:

So far, we have been exploring and emphasizing one's personal walk with Christ through living prayer. However, this passage from Matthew 18 discusses what happens when two or three believers meet. And is there a reason Jesus used two or three and not twelve (he had twelve close disciples)? Let's look at this first.

My sense of an answer comes from what I have experienced in groups, so this could be called the sociological answer. But that does not mean there is no truth in it. (See the Introduction for my email address if you would like to give me some feedback from your experiences.)

One thing Elsie and I have made a habit since we were first married is to have a spoken prayer at any meal we eat together at home (and many times in restaurants). We have found this time of verbally asking God to be with us as we move through our day and face many issues we already know, and some of which we are not aware, to be humbly invigorating and calming. To acknowledge out loud our desire to have God control our day so both of us hear it and can silently affirm it, helps us set a God-centered tone for our day. These prayers are often the beginning to sharing and discussing our lives as they interface with others. That does not mean our finiteness and our propensity to resist God's leading does not haunt us. But, thankfully, God does convict and forgive us.

Another time when praying out loud, between the two of us, is very powerful in our lives is when we are stressed by a bad happening or potential happening or when we have no sense of how God is leading us. Sometimes I awaken after dropping off to sleep because I sense that Elsie is restless from the cares of life. A question asking if she wants to pray (out loud) about it opens a time for us to entreat God and surrender our wills to God. When a young child in our community was struggling with sepsis, we shared many such times. In the end, the disease took the life of the child, but we experienced a fresh time of leaning on God even when we could not understand the "where-for" of this death

As I know from personal experience (and many of you do, too), speaking in or to a large group is much different than participating in a discussion with two or three people. Often, we even use different words for these two experiences—speaking to a group and conversing with a few others. With a few persons talking together, each one must pay close attention to what others are saying and should try to understand what and why they are saying it. In larger groups, anyone's mind can wonder and thus one may not be paying very good attention to the person talking.

Another issue that arises in large groups is that speakers tend to want to grandstand—be perceived as wise, witty, and informed. In such settings, we also tend to state our position simplistically; sometimes it is as if the speaker is presenting a verbal placard or slogan. In small groups where we give each other time enough to fully explain one's viewpoints, we begin to express and understand nuances that are missed in larger groups.

Now let's apply this experiential knowledge to how we relate best in living prayer in very small groups. First, what should the size of a small prayer group be? Jesus first suggests that it is good if two persons agree on a request they share with God. Then Jesus explains that whenever two or three gathers, he will be there. This slight discrepancy in numbers seems to indicate that these numbers are not precise. This might suggest that ten times these numbers are too large but that maybe two times this size would be all right. The test could be that the group needs to be small enough to really experience living prayer—being in close conversation with God and others while being together.

Several persons and ministries have worked on the concept of such small groups and have named them things like Life Transformation Groups and Huddles. In 1999, Neil Cole published his book, *Cultivating a Life with God: Multiplying Disciples Through Life Transformation Groups*. A Life Transformation Group is composed of two to three persons of the same gender committed to God and to each other. They pledge to weekly read the selected Bible passage, to share in accountability and confession, and to pray for God's work within the group and around the world.

Huddles are typically composed of four to six persons, but sometimes they can be even larger. They have a leader involved in helping the group learn and grow in discipleship and leadership skills. They are usually designed to be less than a year in length. Life Transformation Groups and huddles are not like the traditional small groups found in many churches. The so-named "small groups" are usually for support, caring, and Bible study. They can grow and sub-divide as necessary to keep them from getting too large.

Each of these types of small groups—specialized or traditional—depends upon the participants being committed to God and each other. However, due to its small size and limited mission and time-commitment, Life Transformation Groups are probably closest to what Jesus described here in Matthew 18.

As we meet in small groups, we discover that we can have a unity on things that we are praying about or discussing than we might have imagined. This is "agreeing together" as Jesus described it. However, if one person is not in agreement, then this may suggest that a longer time should be taken to discuss and to pray regarding a situation to fully discern God's leading or to help that one person gain a united sense of God's leading.

Jesus promised that what we pray for will happen, but he does give some prerequisites. Small groups of disciples must agree regarding the situation being considered and must know that Jesus is in their midst. If we are not totally united or if we are not sure which way God is leading, this does not mean we are not good disciples or not Christians. I believe that God lets us have times of uncertainty in order to prepare us for what may happen even though it seems like second best or worse. We should remember that Jesus was crucified, Stephen was stoned, Paul was beaten and shipwrecked, and many believers have suffered terribly over the centuries since Jesus lived among us in human form.

Learning to know God's will means we must walk with him continuously and with a committed small group of other believers. Since we are finite and not perfect, we must seek God's forgiveness and must also forgive others. This accountability and sense of vulnerability is a necessary part of being Jesus disciples. Remember the teaching Jesus gave his disciples on forgiveness, after he taught them how to pray as recorded in the Sermon on the Mount found in Matthew 5.

## TO DO:

Talk with God about how he might be leading you into a committed small group. Contact your pastor or mission leader about such groups. Then consider what changes God may be asking you to make for this to happen, e.g., learning to be open and vulnerable.

# 16

## Prayer Is Thanking God for Fellow Believers

### READ: 1 THESSALONIANS 3:6-10

⁶ But Timothy has just now come to us from you and has brought good news about your faith and love. He has told us that you always have pleasant memories of us and that you long to see us, just as we also long to see you. ⁷ Therefore, brothers and sisters, in all our distress and persecution we were encouraged about you because of your faith. ⁸ For now we really live, since you are standing firm in the Lord. ⁹ How can we thank God enough for you in return for all the joy we have in the presence of our God because of you? ¹⁰ Night and day we pray most earnestly that we may see you again and supply what is lacking in your faith.

### PONDER:

What thoughts and challenges do you hear and affirm in this Scripture?

What questions come to you as you read and pondered this Scripture?

## MORE REFLECTIONS:

Again, I confess that here is a passage that I have often read over the years but have missed the clear point that Paul was making: "Night and day we pray most earnestly . . . " (v. 10). As often as we have seen such passages in Paul's writing, I trust that this is not hyperbole. Paul really means that he is living in prayer continuously. Paul and his small band of church planters was praying that God would let them return to the church in Thessalonica so they could again visit these new Christians and through Paul's teaching ministry make the faith of these brothers and sisters even stronger.

Exploring Paul's first associations with persons in the city of Thessalonica will help us understand Paul's attachment to the church there. Thessalonica was in Macedonia which Paul, in a vision, had been led to enter after being in Asia Minor (present day Turkey). As recorded in Acts 16, Paul and his companions, Silas and Timothy, left Philippi after being put in jail there and experiencing a miraculous intervention resulting in a release from imprisonment. The next stop at a major city was in Thessalonica.

In the first 10 verses of Acts 17, Luke records the interactions that Paul and Silas had in that city. They taught in the synagogue, on several sabbaths, how Jesus was the Messiah promised in the Hebrew Scriptures. Luke then writes that "a large number of God-fearing Greeks and quite a few prominent women" joined some Jews in believing Paul's and Silas's message (v. 4). But it was not long before some other Jews instigated a riot which ended up driving Paul and Silas prematurely out of the city.

Ever since Paul left Thessalonica several months earlier, even while he ministered in Athens and then in Corinth, he was concerned about the fledgling church in the city. So, he sent Timothy on a return visit to check things out. With a glowing report from Timothy, Paul seems to have had a holy desire to make a return visit himself where he could spend some time in fellowship and teaching, particularly since he left so quickly from their city.

In the present passage (in 1 Thessalonians 3), Paul states his thankfulness for them: "How can we thank God enough for you in return for all the joy we have in the presence of our God because of you?" (v. 9). What a wonderful accolade to be given to anyone. Earlier (v. 6), Paul presents an even more special accommodation: "Timothy . . . has brought good news about your faith and love."

When was the last time I talked with God thanking him for the Christian friends he has brought and continues to bring into my life? I have friends from the youth group of the church my family was a part of when I was a teenager. Even though our paths no longer cross very regularly, I want to thank God for the faith I developed as we discussed the Bible and how to apply it in our lives. Even though we do see each other every ten years or so, I don't recall ever thanking them for their profound gift to me of enhancing and testing my faith.

Instead of feeling like we have reneged on God when our minds drift from one topic to another when we are "praying," let's relax and let such moments be ways God can talk to us as we share in "living prayer" with him throughout our days and nights. So, as recent memories and long-ago memories replay in our minds, let's use them as opportunities to thank God for friends and mentors and to talk with God about what they may be going through now. Nurturing such memories can help us remember to get in touch with these persons by email (or gasp, by a card in the regular mail!)

From January 2014 through August 2016, we spent most of our time serving the emerging Mennonite church in Lezhë, Albania, and teaching and assisting at the Lezha Academic Center (now a K–12 school emphasizing English and preparation for university education). We did come back to our US house as physical ailments and school vacations encouraged us to do so during this time.

We were invited to stay on in Lezhë, but my joint problems and Elsie's muscular and joint pains have kept us from returning to Albania. However, our hearts are still there. When we have an opportunity, we try to learn about the current situations in the church and school and try to be supportive in whatever ways we can be. So, when we hear good reports from persons visiting there, we feel just a bit like Paul did for the church in Thessalonica. Recently we were involved in a fundraiser for the school and had an opportunity to visit with two Albania college students studying in the USA. This did make us ache to visit Lezhë again. What we can do until our health is repaired is to talk with God about the students, teachers and staff of the school and the persons involved with the church. This becomes an example of "living prayer."

While this was likely the first letter which Paul had written to a new church in a city in the Roman Empire, he wrote many other letters to such churches. In many of these letters, Paul included a note of thanks and shared that he was praying for them. This can be a model for us. Setting our minds to think about those who have been significant in our journey of faith helps put us in a humble and thankful attitude. During "living prayer" with God, we can acknowledge the gifts God has given us in other believers, and we can let the people involved know what impact they have had on our lives. As Paul wrote in a letter to the young church in Rome, "For I am longing to see you so that I may impart to you some spiritual gift to make you strong, that is, that we may be mutually encouraged by each other's faith, both yours and mine" (Romans 1:11–12 [ISV]).

## TO DO:

Today and tomorrow, make a special effort during your exercise of living prayer to thank God for the persons who have significantly impacted your faith in God. Then write their names down and take time to write a thank you note to at least one of these persons. (Does God's Spirit mean I am to do this, too!)

# 17

# Prayer Is Not a Public Activity

## READ: MATTHEW 6:5-8

[5] "And when you pray, do not be like the hypocrites, for they love to pray standing in the synagogues and on the street corners to be seen by others. Truly I tell you, they have received their reward in full. [6] But when you pray, go into your room, close the door and pray to your Father, who is unseen. Then your Father, who sees what is done in secret, will reward you. [7] And when you pray, do not keep on babbling like pagans, for they think they will be heard because of their many words. [8] Do not be like them, for your Father knows what you need before you ask him.

## PONDER:

What thoughts and challenges do you hear and affirm in this Scripture?

What questions come to you as you read and pondered this Scripture?

## MORE REFLECTIONS:

In chapters two and three we already explored Jesus teaching through what is often referred to as the "Lord's Prayer." In the above passage we are backtracking a bit and looking at the material Matthew recorded directly before writing the sample prayer (6:9–13). Since we know Jesus presented these rather boldly different ideas before the sample prayer, this seems to indicate that the Lord's Prayer was not meant to be used as we do today—as a cultural liturgy. Rather, it was a sample prayer showing what kind of topics we might converse with God about when we practice "living prayer."

As opposite to this view, chapter eight of the *Didache*, an early Christian writing, formalizes when believers should fast and when they should say the Lord's Prayer. Written sometime prior to 400 CD (maybe a first draft as early as the second half of the first century), it commands that Christians do not fast with the hypocrites who fast on Mondays and Thursdays, but we are to fast on Wednesdays and Fridays. Also, we are to say the Lord's Prayer three times a day. It is interesting that the *Didache* was never in the New Testament canon. Apparently, its formalized worship style and questionable authorship were not considered to be binding on all believers; this gives some support to the interpretation of the Lord's Prayer we explore in this book.

Jesus' style of teaching from the Matthew 6 passage above is intriguing. He begins with a description of the behavior of the religious leaders which he does not want his disciples to follow, then he finishes with a description of how the disciples should behave. This is then repeated with a new concept. While I am not sure if I ever tried this technique as a teacher or preacher, it seems to be very effective when I hear it in my head as I read. If you or I must ever give a talk or a sermon at church, we can give this a try.

## Do Not Pray to Be Seen; Instead Pray in Secret.

Whatever else might have been a reason for Jesus to urge us not to design our praying for "public consumption," his main concern was what pride does to us and our relationship to God. No matter how much we can get people to say of us: "Oh, she is such wonderful Christians. Did you hear her prayer this morning?" Or maybe we hear: "That was a wonderful prayer. I wonder how much time he puts into writing out his prayers?" Jesus reminds us that such praise is all the reward we will get. By implication he is saying there is no reward in eternity for such behavior.

Instead of behaving as motivated by pride, we need to find a spot that keeps us out of the public limelight. Jesus uses the metaphor here of a "closet" or "room." But it might be when we are out chopping wood, when we are reading the Bible and pondering its meaning, when we are walking down a crowded urban sidewalk, or when we are drinking a coffee in a shop in Albania. If we have developed a "living prayer" lifestyle, then we will be so connected in conversation with God through the Holy Spirit that we will not take the time to polish a prayer for the public.

There has been a time or two when I have been called upon to offer a public prayer where the venue was not a church building. I clearly remember trying to pull together a prayer that would be acceptable to both those who believed in God as well as those who did not. I pondered whether to write the prayer out or do it extemporaneously. I finally settled on simplicity and adapted a well-known verse penned by Reinhold Niebuhr.

> "God, grant me the serenity to accept the things we cannot change,
> Courage to change the things we can,
> And wisdom to know the difference."

Interestingly, I do not remember anyone complimenting me on that prayer. So, my reward was very small indeed since I doubt there will be a heavenly reward for my process in deciding on the prayer.

However, there have been numerous times where I have chatted with the Spirit of God within me or cried out in agony and found a relief even if nothing about a situation changed except that I was sure God now knew all about it (at least as I saw it!)

## Do Not Pray with Many Words; Simply Ask God for What You Need.

Next Jesus reminded his disciples that praying with many words was not helpful nor preferred by God. Many translations of the Bible use the instruction, "do not babble." The New Revised Standard Version makes it even more plain, "do not heap up empty phrases." The disciples could easily have heard this as an allusion to the contest between Elijah and the priests of Baal recorded in 1 Kings 18:26–29 (ISV). Prior to these verses, the priest of the idol Baal prepared a bull for a sacrifice on the altar and tried to call down fire to burn it up. Following that we read:

> [26] So they took the ox that was given to them, prepared it, and called on the name of Baal from early morning until noon. "Baal! Answer us!" they cried. But there was no response. Nobody answered. So they kept on dancing[d] around the altar that they had made.
> [27] Starting about noon, Elijah began to tease them:
> "Shout louder!
> "He's a god, so maybe he's busy.
> "Maybe he's relieving himself.
> "Maybe he's busy someplace.
> "Maybe he's taking a nap and somebody needs to wake him up."
> [28] So the prophets of Baal[e] cried even louder and slashed themselves with swords and lances until their blood gushed out all over them, as was their custom.
> [29] They kept on raving right through midday and until it was time to offer the evening sacrifice, but there was still no response. Nobody answered, and nobody paid attention.

Then Elijah prepared his assigned bull for an evening sacrifice and even asked some strong men to fill four jars of water and pour the liquid on the altar and slain bull until water filled a trench that had been dug around the altar. Elijah then prayed a simple prayer that informed God about the situation and what Elijah needed so that the people would know that Yahweh (the LORD) was their true God (v. 36–37). The author of 1 Kings then writes, "Right then the Lord's fire fell and consumed the burnt offering, the wood, the stones, the dust, and even the water that was in the trench!" (v. 38 [ISV]).

So, the disciples would have heard Jesus loud and clear in his comment about not using babble to get in touch with God. All we must do is to spell out the situation to God. Even that is not for God's sake but for ours. Probably each of us has experienced the relief and encouragement that comes during trying experiences when we share about them with a close friend. God is a very close friend. God loves us with true agape love. So, sharing relieves us of the worry and concern that we may be carrying with regards to our problem situations. God is always already with us at these times. We do not have to work to wake God up or to get the attention of God.

## Summary

As soon as we prepare a prayer to share in public, we have lost at least some of our honesty in relating to God on a one-on-one basis. In fact, might Jesus in this passage be instructing his disciples to completely stay away from public prayer? I feel strongly that is a valid interpretation.

## TO DO:

The next time you share a public prayer, try to analyze your internal responses. Are you tempted to want to do it "right" so that others will praise your praying ability? As an antidote, spend time today in living prayer with the Spirit—in a quiet way share your deepest feelings with God and listen and feel the response that God gives.

# 18

## Prayer Is Letting the Holy Spirit Speak for Us

### READ: ROMANS 8:22-27

<sup>22</sup> We know that the whole creation has been groaning as in the pains of childbirth right up to the present time. <sup>23</sup> Not only so, but we ourselves, who have the firstfruits of the Spirit, groan inwardly as we wait eagerly for our adoption to sonship, the redemption of our bodies. <sup>24</sup> For in this hope we were saved. But hope that is seen is no hope at all. Who hopes for what they already have? <sup>25</sup> But if we hope for what we do not yet have, we wait for it patiently.

<sup>26</sup> In the same way, the Spirit helps us in our weakness. We do not know what we ought to pray for, but the Spirit himself intercedes for us through wordless groans. <sup>27</sup> And he who searches our hearts knows the mind of the Spirit, because the Spirit intercedes for God's people in accordance with the will of God.

## PONDER:

What thoughts and challenges do you hear and affirm in this Scripture?

What questions come to you as you read and pondered this Scripture?

## MORE REFLECTIONS:

Paul, writing to the believers in Rome whom he had not yet met at the time of writing to them, in the passage for today was reminding them of what they could look forward to and what they already had as a taste of what their lives would be like after death.

All of creation, including humans, are groaning because we have not yet been restored to the order that God meant for his creation to have. This perfection is referred to in Genesis 1 with these words repeated several times after God's creative acts, "And God saw that it was good." Even though each of these steps of creation may have taken millions of years to complete, there was a goodness about how they interacted with each other and how they followed God's design.

Paul is first reminding us that God originally had a perfect plan for all of creation, but then by inference Paul acknowledges that this plan went awry. In fact, things went so far out of balance and away from its purpose that Paul suggests we are experiencing such intense existential pain like what a mother experiences at the birth of one of her children. We continue in this pain because we know that the redemption of our physical bodies is going to happen one day. And we live in hope for that day to come, and we hope sooner than later.

The writer of Isaiah 2:4 (ISV) understands what we are hoping for when he wrote:

> "He will judge between the nations,
> and will render verdicts for the benefit of many.
> "They will beat their swords into plowshares,
> and their spears into pruning hooks;

nations will not raise swords against nations,
and they will not learn warfare anymore.

In fact, what is interesting about this poetry is that it is repeated in part or in whole twice in the Old Testament. Joel 3:10 twists our usual wording of this idea on its head: "Beat your plowshares into swords." But a century later, both Isaiah and Micah (4:3) author the verses in the usual form above. Might this be indicative of progressive revelation? Joel seems more nationalistic, but Isaiah and Micah are beginning to understand that God is establishing a global kingdom that is above politics.

The Old Testament prophets were communicators of God's judgement to come on Israel for the sins of its people, but they were also persons of hope as they wrote and preached about the promised Messiah. In the New Testament, Jesus' close disciples and other writers were also attuned to Godly hope as they were speaking from the other side of our Savior's birth, life, death, resurrection, and ascension back to Father God. Hope in the New Testament referred to the expected second coming of the Messiah, but it was hope and not a given. Paul urged the Roman believers to wait patiently in hope, and this is our goal, too.

So, what does this have to do with prayer? Paul says that just as the Holy Spirit is the firstfruits of the new covenant God made with his children after Jesus' time here on Earth, "we wait eagerly for our adoption to sonship, the redemption of our bodies" (v. 23b). As the Spirit living inside of our personhood is the earnest payment for the redemption of our physical bodies, so the Spirit joining us in "living prayer" is the promissory note given believers as a person who can intercede for us and our concerns.

This intercession is accomplished at times by groanings we do not understand. At times we understand what our spirit hungers for in our lives, and at other times we need the deeper penetration of the Holy Spirit into our lives such that later we can say, "Yes, God!" In faith and hope, we trust that the Spirit intercedes on our behalf according to God's will even when we do not know or understand that will.

After four operations to replace both of my hip joints, I understand hoping for the physical restoration of our bodies. (OK, four is not the same as two; my left hip joint had to be replaced three times within two and a half years because the metal of the artificial joint and the bone did not meld well.) And my spirit has often groaned when I did not understand what God was doing with the brokenness of my life and the lives of those around me. From the time I was in my mid-teen years until the day of her death, my mother struggled with mental illness. This meant that as her children, we also struggled to understand what this sickness was all about. I'm sure Dad also shared many groanings and tears with the Spirit of God within him. I do not claim to understand why Mom was sick this way, but I live in faith that God has now brought healing to her and in in the process of bringing healing to those of us who were around her. As I continue to walk in "living prayer," I walk in hope that the Spirit will continue to intercede for me from moment to moment my whole life through.

We are looking forward to our promised physical restoration which has not yet fully happened, but in the meantime as we groan in our spiritual selves, we discover that the Holly Spirit also shares our prayers with God through our wordless groans. We hope for what is not yet ours, and with wonderful abandonment, we trust that God hears us and is leading us according to the divine plan.

## TO DO:

The next time you find that you don't even know how to pray, listen to your groans trusting that God through the Spirit is listening. So, over the next few days open your heart and ears to hear the groans that those around you might be sharing with God. Sometimes he wants us to be his ears, heart, and hands.

# 19

## Prayer Is Connecting with God through Other's Words

### READ: PSALM 51:7-13

[7] Cleanse me with hyssop, and I will be clean;
   wash me, and I will be whiter than snow.
[8] Let me hear joy and gladness;
   let the bones you have crushed rejoice.
[9] Hide your face from my sins
   and blot out all my iniquity.
[10] Create in me a pure heart, O God,
   and renew a steadfast spirit within me.
[11] Do not cast me from your presence
   or take your Holy Spirit from me.
[12] Restore to me the joy of your salvation
   and grant me a willing spirit, to sustain me.
[13] Then I will teach transgressors your ways,
   so that sinners will turn back to you.

## PONDER:

What thoughts and challenges do you hear and affirm in this Scripture?

What questions come to you as you read and pondered this Scripture?

## MORE REFLECTIONS:

While God wants to hear our own thoughts (praises, laments, and petitions), there are times that the words of others can connect us with God in special ways. This Psalm does this for me. When I again find that I have failed God and/or others and need to ask God to turn away from my sin because it disgusts even me, then I can trust that God will wash me and make me cleaner than snow.

On one level, I do not want to identify too closely with this psalm. After all, King David apparently wrote this as a confession after Nathan the prophet pointed out his sin of committing adultery with Bathsheba and then murder by having her husband, who was a soldier, put in the frontlines so that he would be killed and David could marry the pregnant Bathsheba. David could do these things because he was the most powerful person in the political structure of Israel. (See 2 Samuel 11 for more of the story.)

But after wanting to distance myself from David and sin, the Holy Spirit points out to my spirit that all sin is disobeying God— damaging that loving relationship. So, it does not matter what the sin is, it still means I am committing a sin. In this case the solution is clear but not always simple. I must willing return close to God and seek and accept his love and forgiveness. When we get closer to God in living prayer, then it becomes harder to hide our sin and act as if we are perfect and have it all together.

I like the way the writer of 1 John 2:1–2 (ISV) puts it. "My little children, I'm writing these things to you so that you might not sin. Yet if anyone does sin, we have an advocate with the Father—Jesus, the Messiah, one who is righteous. It is he who is the atoning sacrifice for our sins, and not for ours only, but also for the whole world's." The author is addressing believers ("my dear children"), so the sin he is writing about for which we need an advocate is not the sinful nature we have apart from God but rather the sins we commit as believers when we fail to follow Jesus as his disciple. We are not God and thus we are not perfect. But the atoning sacrifice of Jesus death and resurrection still is what is needed to cover our sins.

The writer of the letter we know as Hebrews, after listing and describing persons of faith, whom we can emulate in chapter eleven, begins chapter twelve with a call to seek forgiveness and to learn discipleship (Heb 12:1—2 [ISV]):

> [1] Therefore, having so vast a cloud of witnesses surrounding us, and throwing off everything that hinders us and especially the sin that so easily entangles us, let us keep running with endurance the race set before us, [2] fixing our attention on Jesus, the pioneer and perfecter of the faith, who, in view of the joy set before him, endured the cross, disregarding its shame, and has sat down at the right hand of the throne of God.

Having Jesus as our atoning sacrifice does not mean we can do whatever we wish, but rather it provides the hope and motivation for us to live as Jesus' disciples, running the race of faithfulness to completion. The life of a disciple is not a one-time decision; it is a journey we must run always focusing on Jesus who ran it before us and now waits for us at the side of our Father God.

Going back to Psalm 51, I'll focus in on verse 10. "Create in me a pure heart, O God, and renew a steadfast spirit within me." I can imagine a picture as I ponder this again and again. I am walking with Jesus on a leisurely hike in the spring of the year through a wooded area. We are noticing the many small and medium-sized wildflowers in bloom. Until it strikes me anew, and I cannot seem to look Jesus in the eye. I am remembering how I have failed him today—getting curt with Elsie and blaming her for what was clearly an accident and how I was too busy to really stop to listen to a neighbor expressing her grief to me again. So, I utter the words of Psalm 51:10 again, "Create in me a clean heart, [my] God.." Jesus puts his arm over my shoulder and says, "You are forgiven! You are here in Paradise with me now." Your picture will be different than mine, but both pictures will show the love God has for us through Jesus Christ.

There are clearly times when we will share the words written by others when these words clearly connect with us on an emotional level. But we should not let others' words always take the place of us forming our own deep thoughts and groans in living prayer with God.

## TO DO:

Today write the first draft of a prayer that expresses your need for God's forgiveness through Christ. This is not to show off your perfection as a believer in Christ, but rather it is to describe your "living prayer" relationship with God. Put it somewhere safe from being lost and hone it over the next few days as you voice it each day. Here is one of my offerings to God. It is in free verse form. You might prefer more words in a rhyming form or a haiku. Whatever you use, the form is simply a vehicle for sharing your thoughts in openness and vulnerability with God in living prayer.

REDEMPTION
by R. L. Bowman, © 2019

Sinned
again
Failed
again
Forgive
me
Wash
me
God
yes
Thank
you!

# 20

# Prayer Is Seeking God's Wisdom

## READ: JAMES 1:5-8

⁵ If any of you lacks wisdom, you should ask God, who gives generously to all without finding fault, and it will be given to you. ⁶ But when you ask, you must believe and not doubt, because the one who doubts is like a wave of the sea, blown and tossed by the wind. ⁷ That person should not expect to receive anything from the Lord. ⁸ Such a person is double-minded and unstable in all they do.

## PONDER:

What thoughts and challenges do you hear and affirm in this Scripture?

What questions come to you as you read and pondered this Scripture?

## MORE REFLECTIONS:

How many times have you wanted and sought the wisdom of God! But exactly what is it you wanted from God? Do you need to know how to do calculus or which experiments to do to earn your MS in engineering? Might you want to know how to get your extended family to live at peace or how to convince your brother that becoming a child of God through faith in Jesus Christ is the only way to God?

The New Testament writers use "*sophia*" (σοφία), translated "wisdom" in our English translations, to refer to both knowledge and ways of behaving as defined by the culture and world around us and the insights and understanding of life that can only come from God. Paul in his first letter to the Corinthian believers clearly used wisdom in both ways.

> [20] Where is the wise person? Where is the scholar? Where is the philosopher of this age? God has turned the wisdom of the world into nonsense, hasn't he? [21] For since, in the wisdom of God, the world through its wisdom did not know God, God was pleased to save those who believe through the nonsense of our preaching. [22] Jews ask for signs, and Greeks look for wisdom, [23] but we preach the Messiah crucified. He is a stumbling block to Jews and nonsense to gentiles, [24] but to those who are called, both Jews and Greeks, the Messiah is God's power and God's wisdom. [25] For God's nonsense is wiser than human wisdom, and God's weakness is stronger than human strength (1 Cor 1:20–24 [ISV]).

As followers of Jesus the Messiah, we are seeking God's wisdom and not the wisdom of this world . We should note that the Greek word for wisdom (*sophia*) has come into English with primarily a negative meaning, that is, a sophist is a person who is a clever thinker but does it with false premises.

Many times, the New Testament writers are not explicit about whether they are writing about God's wisdom or the wisdom of the world. But from the context, we can usually determine what is meant. Here in James 1, the writer is obviously referring only to God's wisdom. What else would we go to God to obtain?

Wisdom is an important idea in Jewish (Old Testament) theology. One of the major divisions of the Hebrew Scriptures is called "wisdom literature" and encompasses Job, Psalms (but not all psalms are wisdom literature), Proverbs, Ecclesiastes, the Song of Songs (Song of Solomon), and two books in the Apocrypha section of the English Bible, the Book of Wisdom and Sirach (Ecclesiasticus). Many times, wisdom is personified as a woman in this literature: "Out in the open wisdom calls aloud, she raises her voice in the public square; on top of the wall she cries out, at the city gate she makes her speech" (Proverbs 1: 20–21). In the gospel of Matthew, which was written primarily for Jewish believers, Jesus also refers to wisdom as a female: "But wisdom is proved right by her deeds" (Matt 11:19).

I very much need wisdom from God. Just now Elsie and I were rather intensely talking about some mix-ups regarding some prescriptions that needed to be refilled. How can I apologize and at the same time help us to converse plainly and not rely on unshared assumptions we both make? Also, last evening I felt down. I do not know how to handle a situation where I had helped a person come up with a more precise procedure for doing a financial calculation, but when we met as a committee, my calculation was not presented nor acknowledged.

I need wisdom to know how to deal with my selfishness but also to know when to be assertive. Maybe I already have this wisdom, that is, to walk in living prayer with the Spirit of God gives me all the significance I need. To be loved by God is more than we can ever ask for. So, we can share discouragements and frustrations with God trusting that from this interaction we will learn the wisdom of God.

God also knows what we need. In the same evening as the above occurred, I had a quick answer to my request for wisdom from God on another topic. The end of the month was going to be here in one more day, and I needed a creative idea for a new monthly cartoon for "Little Rich's Questions" ( https://richardlbowman.

com/LRQ/ ). I had pondered this off and on for the past two days, but this evening right after I shared this with God my reactions to the committee work, a clear and exciting idea came to me for the cartoon. Can I thank God for both experiences knowing that wisdom is available even when it is not always obvious?

This passage in James also raises a question in my mind whenever I read these verses. That is, how do I know if I have enough faith to believe that God will give me wisdom when I ask for it? Begin with what you do have faith to believe. Do you believe that God exists? If so, then by inference, you already know some characteristics of God. Is God love? Is God perfect? (If God is not perfect, then how can he be God? Now we are getting into apologetics, but maybe that is where we are already.) Are you perfect? No! Therefore, are you a sinner? Do you believe that a loving God has provided a way for us to be forgiven and become one of his children through the birth, life (teaching and example), death, resurrection, and ascension of Jesus Christ?

I am assuming that believers are reading this book on prayer with God, so all you answered "yes" to the last question above. And thus, you know that you do have a lot of faith in God. Pondering what you do believe about God leads directly to faith that God *can* provide wisdom to us, and from there it is not too big of a jump to having faith that God *will* give us wisdom if we ask for it.

In the end, it comes down to what the man who had a son with characteristics we would most likely call epilepsy today told Jesus. (See Mark 9:14–29.) The disciples were trying to cast out this bad spirit but could not. Jesus came down from the mountain where the Transfiguration had just occurred and saw a mass of people arguing. Jesus and the boy's father discuss belief with the father responding, "I do believe; help me overcome my unbelief!" (Mark 9:24b). These are the words I often share with God in living prayer.

A close example happened today. We attended Sunday services at a church we had not been at recently but where we knew the people, including recent pastors, very well. This evening, as I reviewed the names of the pastors this church has had while talking with God, I remembered the one that I needed faith to believe God could work with. So, in humility I prayed that God would bring reconciliation for this person and friends and family. So, help us, God.

## TO DO:

As you converse with God today and the next several days, notice the opportunities when you need God's wisdom. Then share this request with God in living prayers along with, "I do believe; help me overcome my unbelief!" Also, notice the times you need to make the distinction between God's wisdom and the world's wisdom, and select God's wisdom whenever it comes to a choice between the two.

# 21

## Prayer Is Tapping into Who God Is

### READ: JOHN 17:20–26

[20] "My prayer is not for them [my disciples] alone. I pray also for those who will believe in me through their message, [21] that all of them may be one, Father, just as you are in me and I am in you. May they also be in us so that the world may believe that you have sent me. [22] I have given them the glory that you gave me, that they may be one as we are one— [23] I in them and you in me—so that they may be brought to complete unity. Then the world will know that you sent me and have loved them even as you have loved me.

[24] "Father, I want those you have given me to be with me where I am, and to see my glory, the glory you have given me because you loved me before the creation of the world.

[25] "Righteous Father, though the world does not know you, I know you, and they know that you have sent me. [26] I have made you known to them, and will continue to make you known in order that the love you have for me may be in them and that I myself may be in them."

## PONDER:

What thoughts and challenges do you hear and affirm in this Scripture?

What questions come to you as you read and pondered this Scripture?

## MORE REFLECTIONS:

This part of what is often called, Jesus' High Priestly Prayer, is well-known to most believers in Christ, the son of God. It is a call, a prayer, for unity among Jesus' disciples as there is unity between Jesus the Messiah and God the Father. While this idea of unity is familiar, it has been hard for the disciples of Christ to attain it in the centuries that have passed since Christ ascended back to be with God the Father.

Why is this so hard for us? Might it be because we have missed this call to be in Christ such that we are "living prayer" as a way of life rather than just praying as a series of events? The type of "in-ness" described by Jesus here is a oneness in conversation (a life of prayer), purpose, and action. Jesus knew why he was living here on Earth. He was the Messiah God had sent to live and die on Earth and then to be resurrected and go back to Father God.

The Gospel of Mark seems to specialize in recording how often Jesus predicted his death and how many times his disciples did not understand him. In Mark 9:30–32 (ISV), it is recorded how Jesus told his disciples a second time about his death.

> [30] Then they left that place and passed through Galilee. Jesus[z] didn't want anyone to find out about it, [31] because he was teaching his disciples, "The Son of Man will be betrayed into human hands. They will kill him, but after being dead for three days he will be raised." [32] They didn't understand what this statement meant, and they were afraid to ask him.

God the Father and Jesus Christ agreed on this purpose and action. Jesus knew his purpose on Earth from clear back at creation, but he described it as God glorifying him because God loved him (v. 24).

As Jesus disciples, we can agree with God about what we are here on Earth to do—to praise God, to serve him, and to share the good news of salvation with others. The particulars of how this will be done might appear cloudy now and as we look to the future, but we trust that God knows how it is going to turn out. God is carrying us through this time, so we will be glorified and thus show the world that God loves us. All of this is to show that Jesus' disciples are united as he and God are.

Jesus prayed that we may be in him and God the Father (v. 21). Then he also said that he wants us to have unity by which he meant that he would be in us and God the Father would be in him. This mutual "in-ness" is awesome. It means that we can share intimately with God our desires, our regrets, our frustrations, and our joys. God can then share gifts of comfort, encouragement, forgiveness, and direction for living.

When Jesus (through God's Spirit) is in us, then God's love is there. So, what does that mean? First, for those of us who struggle with our sinfulness, God's love in us means that we have been granted mercy and grace for living. This is where my mind went as I read this passage once again before writing this devotional. Then as I worked at writing down my thoughts, I realized that Jesus was praying that we would know God's love so deeply that we would want to share it with others so they can know Jesus.

With that understanding tossing itself around in my mind, I found a new question. How does God want me to express his love to others? Jesus must be our example and mentor in how to love others. As we noted in a previous chapter, Jesus Christ came to Earth to be our redeemer. But he also came to teach us how to live as God's children.

If we explore Jesus' last few hours before he was crucified, we see both aspects of God's love he expressed. Matthew 26 records Jesus' comments against using force to solve problems including keeping his crucifixion from happening. An armed group of men came to arrest Jesus.

> <sup>49</sup> So Judas immediately went up to Jesus and said, "Hello, Rabbi!" and kissed him tenderly.
>
> <sup>50</sup> Jesus asked him, "Friend, why are you here?" Then the other men surged forward, took hold of Jesus, and arrested him.
>
> <sup>51</sup> Suddenly, one of the men with Jesus reached out his hand, drew his sword, and struck the high priest's servant, cutting off his ear. <sup>52</sup> Jesus told him, "Put your sword back in its place! Everyone who uses a sword will be killed by a sword. <sup>53</sup> Don't you think that I could call on my Father, and he would send me more than twelve legions of angels now? <sup>54</sup> How, then, would the Scriptures be fulfilled that say this must happen?"
>
> <sup>55</sup> At this point, Jesus asked the crowds, "Have you come out with swords and clubs to arrest me as if I were a bandit? Day after day I sat teaching in the Temple, yet you didn't arrest me. <sup>56</sup> But all of this has happened so that the writings of the prophets might be fulfilled."
>
> Then all the disciples deserted Jesus and ran away (26:50–56 [ISV])."

In verse 53 and 54, Jesus reminds his disciples and the crowd who had come with weapons to arrest him that he had the resources (twelve legions of angels) to have kept him from being arrested. However, this was not God's purpose. Violence breeds more violence, and stopping some actions may invalidate what had been prophesized by godly persons.

But it is also very informative how Jesus addressed the armed crowd. He did not just sit back and act like the proverbial dishrag, but he confronted them about their behavior of carrying out this arrest at night and with an armed crowd. He knew and they knew that if they had done this in the daytime, those who had welcomed Jesus on the Sunday before as he entered Jerusalem on a donkey would have risen to support Jesus, and a riot would probably have ensued.

After Jesus was condemned to death and was hung on the cross where he would suffocate to death, he expressed God's love for one of the criminals who was being put to death next to Jesus (Luke 23:39–43 [ISV]):

> ³⁹ Now one of the criminals hanging there kept insulting him, "You are the Messiah, aren't you? Save yourself . . . and us!"
> ⁴⁰ But the other criminal rebuked him, "Aren't you afraid of God, since you are suffering the same penalty? ⁴¹ We have been condemned justly, because we are getting what we deserve for what we have done, but this man has done nothing wrong." ⁴² Then he went on to plead, "Jesus, remember me when you come into your kingdom!"
> ⁴³ Jesus told him, "I tell you with certainty, today you will be with me in Paradise."

As believers in Jesus as the Christ (Messiah), we also know these encouraging words from Jesus when we came to him the first time as our Savior: "Today you will be with me!" God's love has flowed into our hearts, and we have learned how to live in him and let him live in us. Now we need to keep practicing "living prayer" to continue this journey as his children.

## TO DO:

Today tap into who God is by speaking our deepest thoughts with God and then listening to the deepest thoughts spoken with love to our hearts. Practice this "in-ness"—God in us and we in God. Write down some thoughts at the end of the day how you think this went today.

# 22

# Prayer Is Listening to God Speak to Our Spirits

## READ: PHILIPPIANS 4:4-9

[4] Rejoice in the Lord always. I will say it again: Rejoice! [5] Let your gentleness be evident to all. The Lord is near. [6] Do not be anxious about anything, but in every situation, by prayer and petition, with thanksgiving, present your requests to God. [7] And the peace of God, which transcends all understanding, will guard your hearts and your minds in Christ Jesus.

[8] Finally, brothers and sisters, whatever is true, whatever is noble, whatever is right, whatever is pure, whatever is lovely, whatever is admirable—if anything is excellent or praiseworthy—think about such things. [9] Whatever you have learned or received or heard from me, or seen in me—put it into practice. And the God of peace will be with you.

## PONDER:

What thoughts and challenges do you hear and affirm in this Scripture?

What questions come to you as you read and pondered this Scripture?

## MORE REFLECTIONS:

Initially these verses were not in my planning for this book. But when I gave a very condensed version of the topic in a sermon in our congregation this past Sunday, our pastor put verses six and seven at the top of our morning bulletin. I thought this was so appropriate that I just had to add a chapter in the book for this passage written by the Apostle Paul. This time it was our pastor whose words were for me from God. But I need all my Christian brothers and sisters to help me more fully hear God's voice. "Thank you, God, that I am part of your family!"

I was chatting with a friend just a day or so ago about the idea of "living prayer," and we both mentioned how over the years we had found it hard to keep a set time and an active list of situations we wanted to seek God's power to set right. We both acknowledged that we knew this should be life giving and not a life-killing routine but that too often that is what it was. This idea of being in living conversation with God has been a life changer for me, and this friend thought it would be for them, too.

At several places in previous chapters, particularly in chapter eleven, we shared about topics that are very appropriate for our conversations with God's Spirit who abides in Christian believers. "So, in addition to prayers for a person to become a child of God always being a legitimate subject of our conversation with God, prayers for healing and for life to be restored to another person are also good subjects to share with God in living prayer." Here in chapter four of Philippians, Apostle Paul gives us more ideas of situations to be sharing with God in living prayer.

We can rejoice with the Spirit because God has come near to us (v. 4–5). And when we find anxiety-producing situations, we must share those with the God in us. And we need to do this with thanksgiving (v. 6). Thanksgiving for what? To me it is apparent that our thanksgiving arises from the fact that we can and do trust in the God who is close to us.

A metaphor for this is the trust a child has in the adults who care for her. Since Elsie and I have four children and now ten grandchildren, we have had many opportunities to observe a young child being pursued by another child (or teenager), and the young child runs to one of their care-giving adults and clings to this person's leg while peaking around to see if there is still any danger (anyone still following). "God, I am clinging to you. Please continue to be with me."

Paul gives us crucial reassurance in verse seven. Read it above or study how the ISV translation puts it: "Then God's peace, which goes far beyond anything we can imagine, will guard your hearts and minds in union with the Messiah Jesus (Phil 4:7 [ISV])." Again, I am reminded of a small child with their adult protector. But in this case, we cannot truly imagine all that God's peace will bring us.

A few of the ways we can image that God will bring us peace include reduced anxiety, a sense of security, knowledge that someone else is control, joy, the freedom to see the many blessings God has given us such as "raindrops on roses," and thus the ability to truly listen to others. As we listen to others, we will then be in living prayer with God about what we observed and can then hear what, if anything, God wants us to do to care for them. When we are anxious and focused on our own problems (just perceived or real), it is hard for us to truly be open to and care for others in need or to even rejoice with them.

I am reminded of Jesus interaction with the children whose parent had brought them to Jesus for a blessing but whom the disciples were turning away.

> [13] Some people were bringing little children to Jesus to have him touch them. But the disciples rebuked those

who brought them. [14] When Jesus saw this, he became furious and told them, "Let the little children come to me, and stop keeping them away, because the kingdom of God belongs to people like these. [15] I tell all of you with certainty, whoever doesn't receive the kingdom of God as a little child will never enter it." [16] Then after he had hugged the children, he tenderly blessed them as he laid his hands on them (Mark 10:13–16 [ISV]).

It is this kind of caring, protective love that we find when we get close to Jesus and are in living prayer with God. This is so important that all three synoptic gospels describe this instance and use almost the same words. Thus, see also Matt 19:13–15 and Luke 18:15–17. So, we need to enter a relationship with Jesus as the little children did—seeking God out and letting his Spirit hug us. What a wonderful metaphor.

Paul finally used words that he felt described what God would give us to think about as we get near to God. We should think on whatever is true, noble, right, pure, lovely, admirable, excellent, or praiseworthy (v. 8). He even urges his listeners to practice those things that they have "learned or received or heard from me, or seen in me." My hope is that God is working so closely and deeply with me that others (friends, children, grandchildren, and strangers) will want to know the God I love and to follow in my footsteps. I sure do not feel worthy to offer this to anyone, but if God directs them and me, then I will try to follow.

Living prayer is listening to and conversing with God about all the events of life and then to know his nearness so that my anxiety will be changed to thoughts that come from the peace God gives to us as his children

## TO DO:

Today and tomorrow trust in the God who is close to you and try to leave your anxieties with God's Spirit so that you can experience the peace from God. Then focus on the good thoughts that arise from this living prayer conversation.

# 23

# Prayer Is Loving Our Enemies

## READ: MATTHEW 5:43-48

[43] "You have heard that it was said, 'Love your neighbor and hate your enemy.' [44] But I tell you, love your enemies and pray for those who persecute you, [45] that you may be children of your Father in heaven. He causes his sun to rise on the evil and the good, and sends rain on the righteous and the unrighteous. [46] If you love those who love you, what reward will you get? Are not even the tax collectors doing that? [47] And if you greet only your own people, what are you doing more than others? Do not even pagans do that? [48] Be perfect, therefore, as your heavenly Father is perfect.

## PONDER:

What thoughts and challenges do you hear and affirm in this Scripture?

What questions come to you as you read and pondered this Scripture?

## MORE REFLECTIONS:

This passage is from the Sermon on the Mount from which we looked at several passages already. Jesus follows the teaching technique he used several times in that grouping of instructions for his disciples. He quotes something they may have heard either in the synagogues or in the general culture around them and then puts his more complete spin on this piece of wisdom.

Many scholars point out that the Torah (the first five books of the Old Testament) does not say to "hate your enemies." Leviticus 19:18 does say, " . . . love your neighbor as yourself," which is apparently aimed at fellow Jews. Backing up a verve we read, "Do not hate a fellow Israelite in your heart." However, it appears that separatist groups of Jews in Jesus day (for example, the Zealots and the Dead Sea community in Qumran) had been extending this rule to include hatred of the Roman enemies. Remember that Jesus had a Zealot among his twelve closest disciples, Simon the Zealot (Matthew 10:4, Mark 3:18, Luke 6:15, and Acts 1:13).

So, Jesus is taking issue with a popular saying in the culture around him and is reminding his disciples that God loves all people. We should love our enemies and pray for them. As we remember that in this same group of teachings, Jesus taught his disciples to get into a secret (away from crowds) place to converse intimately with God (Matthew 6:5–8). This is quite the change from current teachings of Jesus' day. To take time away from people and the responsibilities of our day to pray to God was not just a trivial one sentence prayer for our enemies. When we converse with God, our time together on one or more topics will be extensive. So, it must be with our prayers for our enemies.

Jesus explains that when we love our enemies, we are showing that we are truly children of God the Father. God send sun and rain equally on the righteous and the unrighteous. He then extends this reasoning to say that if we love only those who will love us in return, then we are no different than the tax collectors. The persons who collected taxes for the Roman occupation forces were often grouped together with other evil people. The Pharisees

condemned Jesus for eating with "tax collectors and sinners."
Even though Jesus uses "tax collectors" as a synonym for the low-
est group of his day, he often associated with them. Luke records,
"Now the tax collectors and sinners were all gathering around to
hear Jesus. But the Pharisees and the teachers of the law muttered,
'This man welcomes sinners and eats with them'" (Matt 15:1–2).

When was the last time people talked badly about us because
we associated with sinners? That is something I need to talk with
God about as we share in "living prayer." How do I know with
whom God is leading me to interact? Who is it who are called "sinners" (outcasts, people from across the tracks, lower class persons)
in the culture in which I am living?

In a visit to Mumbai, India, more than a decade ago, I drove
past the "Dhobi Ghat" where hundreds of washer workers do their
tasks. Some of us where appalled by the tour guide's comment that
each person does best when they know the position in society they
are to fill and do that. But do Western cultures have a more subtle
class structure. Jesus' goal was to bring his good news to all groups
and thus tear down unhealthy class structures.

A question that comes up regularly with Christians from
North America who go into "majority world" cultures is: How do I
know what to do when I meet beggars? During our time in Belize
(1970–73) as a missionary pastor couple, we met a few beggars
along the street. We were convinced that God loves everyone including the beggars, but what was the best way to show God's love.
Occasionally we gave some money, and one time I took the person
to a local hamburger-and-milk-shake restaurant to get a meal.

On other occasions we had persons stop by and ask for
money or a job. I remember the first time we left a man cut the
grass in our yard with a machete and paid him for doing the job.
Some other Americans thought we were just encouraging the man
to come back. During the three years we lived in Belize City, that
man did find us again even though we had moved. Sometimes we
just talked, but sometimes he did ask for money for some stated
need. Even though we were on a subsistence wage, all our medical

costs were covered. Thus, we were richer than our friend by far, and a minor redirection of wealth seemed the least we could do.

While living in Albania (2014–16) there were several beggars who would regularly hold their hand out for a contribution. When it was young children asking for money for food, sometimes we gave them the left-over pizza we were carrying home from a restaurant, or we would take them to a shop to buy some bread. This was our small step toward authentic sharing. These situations clearly show our need to be in living prayer with the Spirit to learn God's wisdom for us in these matters.

There have been several good books written on the bad effects of badly given money. Before living in a cross-cultural setting, it would be good to read and ponder the ideas in such books. Even secular organizations are realizing the unexpected harm that can come from our careless distribution of aid. NPR published a news article entitled, "Advice to Parachuting Docs: Think Before You Jump into Poor Countries," regarding a new a position paper produced by the American College of Physicians. Search for the NPR articles at www.npr.org to see where it its current located.

God does want us to love those around us, and if we do not struggle in living prayer with how to best show God's love, then maybe the Spirit of God should shake us up to see the many needs around us—physical, emotional, spiritual, financial, and racial inequality. Remember that we live in a global world, so our neighbors are those who live anywhere in the world. For more to think about, reread Jesus' parable of the Good Samaritan (Luke 10:15–37).

This section of the Sermon on the Mount we read at the beginning of this chapter and the two ancillary scriptural passages presented in the previous chapter are some of the foundational texts for my personal belief in non-violence. When I graduated from college in 1970, the Vietnam War was still in high gear as far as the US military was concerned. I was a convinced non-resistant Christian, but there were still a few questions I had to ponder and answer during my four years in college. Was refusing to register for the draft a legitimate Christian response to war? Was it OK to participate in demonstrations against war if some of the persons involved were not Christians? Was it acceptable for a Christian pacifist to accept an orderly job in a mental hospital just a couple of hours away from home when friends in the military may end up thousands of miles from their home?

For myself, I felt it was fine to register for the draft, but I could not serve in the military even as a chaplain. Accepting an alternate service job too close to home did not seem to be a sacrificial enough response to war, so Elsie and I (we were married in June after I graduated in May) asked our mission board if they had any openings for overseas service we could fit in to do. So, we were sent to Belize City where I pastored a local emerging national Mennonite church. Learning to live non-violently and at peace in various settings is still a goal of my journeying with Christ in living prayer.

## TO DO:

If living sacrificially and non-violently, loving others around the globe, and praying for our enemies is new to you, then study the passages in these last two chapters and in living prayer seek God's guidance. Whatever your perspective is on war, spend time in living prayer to seek God's will on how to help those who are homeless and begging or the immigrants among us and at our borders.

# 24

## Prayer Is a Healing Activity

### READ: JAMES 5:13–18

[13] Is anyone among you in trouble? Let them pray. Is anyone happy? Let them sing songs of praise. [14] Is anyone among you sick? Let them call the elders of the church to pray over them and anoint them with oil in the name of the Lord. [15] And the prayer offered in faith will make the sick person well; the Lord will raise them up. If they have sinned, they will be forgiven. [16] Therefore confess your sins to each other and pray for each other so that you may be healed. The prayer of a righteous person is powerful and effective.

[17] Elijah was a human being, even as we are. He prayed earnestly that it would not rain, and it did not rain on the land for three and a half years. [18] Again he prayed, and the heavens gave rain, and the earth produced its crops.

### PONDER:

What thoughts and challenges do you hear and affirm in this Scripture?

What questions come to you as you read and pondered this Scripture?

## MORE REFLECTIONS:

Basically, anything or everything can be talked about with God in living prayer. While this topic has not been discussed explicitly, if one peruses what we have talked about, a list of some acceptable topics will quickly emerge. God's will be done on Earth. Crying for forgiveness. Letting the Holy Spirit share our groans with God. Seeking wisdom. Loving our enemies. Many more!

But none of these chapters have especially emphasized praying for healing which is what we want to spend the day thinking about. You and I have probably experienced God's healing touch, or we know of others who have. So, the possibility of healing is often not the tension point but rather how do we know when God wants us to ask for it, and how do we know that he will heal or not. At 70 years of age, I can vouch that these questions will remain for our Earthly lives. I can also assure all of us that God does heal but not necessarily in our way nor our timing.

Here are important parts of my life's timeline. After three years in Belize and one year getting my MA in physics from Kent State University, Ohio, Elsie and I moved to Corvallis, Oregon, where I began my studies toward a PhD in biophysics at Oregon State University in the fall of 1974. One day in class in the spring of 1975, I noticed that if I closed my right eye, all I could see was very blurry. It was a rather quick change and one that was there each day. Once I got to see an ophthalmologist, the damage was already done—scar tissue had formed in my retina when the body fought off a histoplasmosis infection. The scars were spread at a low density across the retinas in both eyes. However, in the left eye scarring had occurred directly on the macular region wiping out my central vision there. At least the situation was stable.

Just over a year later, the situation became unstable. New blood vessels that had grown to support some scarring near the macular region in my right eye began breaking open and bleeding.

Most eye doctors did not have lasers in that time period. So, I was sent to the medical school in Portland, but the doctors there did not want to do any cauterization with a laser because they knew they would be damaging the underlying optic nerve with the laser in order to stop the bleeding of the small vessels above it. I was finally sent to Palo Alto, California, where there was a group of eye doctors working only on retinal issues. Dr. Hunter Little examined the eye and its state of bleeding and did photocoagulation with a laser to stop the bleeding.

The above is only a description of the medical part of my care. Elsie and I and our families and friends from across the US were all praying for God's healing of my retina. To this day I thank God for his healing touch through Dr. Little and his laser and through God's touch on my physical body. I cannot sort these out into neat categories, but I do know that the level of vision I have had for many decades now and the little damage done to my optic nerve are all well above the doctors' and my expectations. We praise God for that. At the worst time, I could only read the largest headlines in a newspaper. Since the last photocoagulation in June 1986, I have been able to read textbooks, articles and papers generated by administrators as I functioned as a college professor of physics. I do have eyeglasses with a large amount of magnification, but at least I can read at some level.

So, how do I summarize my eyesight experience. As a Christian believer, I know that God has healed me this far, and I have so much to thank him for as I read lots of material through my Kindle with large font size and my computer with low resolution (so that the fonts are large). But this is not the storyline for my non-Christian friends. My experience is not a proof that God exists, but if one already knows that God exists and cares for his people, then my experiences is verification of faith in God.

The writer of James, in this passage, presents specifications for the practice of anointing with oil as carried out by many Mennonite congregations and churches of other denominations. I am thankful for the many experiences of prayer for healing by a small group of believers and through the practice of anointing with oil and prayer for healing. Both have resulted in healing at times, and at times neither practice has led to healing. A study of the example of Elijah's prayers leading to a drought and then again to adequate rain for crops reminds us that such prayers are only guaranteed to lead to success when we know for certain that God is leading us into such situations. It might help for us to remember that right after the Mt. Carmel incident described in chapter seventeen Elijah became very discouraged and ran away into the desert because he was sure he was the only follower of Yahweh left. This was far from the truth, but it is what Elijah thought.

So, our talking with God in living prayer about opportunities in which we need God's healing touch is a good practice to enhance our faith in possibilities of God's action and our trusting that God is still in control even if healing is not the outcome. The practice of anointing the sick with oil and with prayers by church leaders following a period of self-examination and confession of sins will also bring healing to our spiritual selves even if not to our physical bodies. For me personally, the time leading up to my various joint replacement surgeries have been excellent times for me to talk with God about the state of my relationship with him. I have confessed sins that keep haunting me and expressed trust that I am willing to accept whatever outcome there will be from my surgery. I am not seeking death, but when death comes, I want to be prepared for it.

## TO DO:

As you meet sickness or weakness this week, whether physical, emotional, or spiritual, talk with God in faith, confessing your sins and seeking his healing. Perhaps such times are opportunities to practice anointing with oil and prayer. At least consider sharing these with a few other believers who are close to you in prayer.

# 25

## Prayer Is Living
## in Conversation with God

### READ: 1 THESSALONIANS 1:1-6

<sup>1</sup> Paul, Silas and Timothy,

To the church of the Thessalonians in God the Father and the Lord Jesus Christ: Grace and peace to you.

<sup>2</sup> We always thank God for all of you and continually mention you in our prayers. <sup>3</sup> We remember before our God and Father your work produced by faith, your labor prompted by love, and your endurance inspired by hope in our Lord Jesus Christ.

<sup>4</sup> For we know, brothers and sisters loved by God, that he has chosen you, <sup>5</sup> because our gospel came to you not simply with words but also with power, with the Holy Spirit and deep conviction. You know how we lived among you for your sake. <sup>6</sup> You became imitators of us and of the Lord, for you welcomed the message in the midst of severe suffering with the joy given by the Holy Spirit.

## PONDER:

What thoughts and challenges do you hear and affirm in this Scripture?

What questions come to you as you read and pondered this Scripture?

## MORE REFLECTIONS:

Paul in verse two gives the believers in Thessalonica an accolade that any of us would welcome from a friend. "We always thank God for all of you and continually mention you in our prayers." They were affirmed by their labor in love and faith in Jesus the Messiah and were always being mentioned in Paul's conversations with God. Paul's living prayers for the Thessalonian believers were not just thanksgivings for their faith, but I am sure he also was petitioning God on their behalf for more faith and opportunities to share that faith and for safety, spiritually and physically.

Recently a friend who had been serving as a teacher in Albania where we had served back in 2014–16, told us how much we are loved and mentioned in that school and the local church. This affirmation was very gratifying, making our time and effort there to have some level of significance. In fact, this information was clearly a gentle push encouraging us to return for a short visit.

With this good news coming to us and with Paul's example recorded here in 1 Thessalonians 1, I am challenged to examine my life to see how affirming I have been of friends and family in their walk with God. My dad, who turned 91 in the middle of 2019, has been an inspiration to me in how to live and walk as a child of God through Jesus Christ. I have been trying to learn how to let him know by words and deeds how much he means to me and has been used by God in my life. The question then becomes: Are there other persons whom I have failed to continuously pray for in my conversations with God and whom I have not thanked for their effect on my life?

So, what does it mean to be in continuous conversation with God? Surely, we do not talk to God like an uninhibited three-year-old does to her parents during her awake time. In fact, we have learned in our study in this book that babbling to God is not honest and open praying. Should it be more like the relationship between a husband and a wife such that as they are both helping their two children with homework in the evening, the husband says to his wife in passing, "I love you"? Or maybe like a husband and wife taking a driving trip to a location some hours away from their home? They chat with each other about a few deep problems they are facing but also bring each other up to date on some less-serious happenings in their lives. It has to do with the possibility and the willingness to share about all the situations of life.

Our living prayer life with God gives us significance not so much because of what we share, or even get from God, but because we can know that in love God has chosen us to be his children, to be part of his global family. As Paul, Silas, and Timothy remind the Thessalonians how the three of them had lived in their city, can we also remind those with whom we shared the gospel (good news) of a relationship with God through Christ that " . . . our gospel came to you not simply with words but also with power, with the Holy Spirit and deep conviction. You know how we lived among you for your sake. You became imitators of us and of the Lord . . . " (v. 5–6)?

Do we share the good news so that we can count how many persons became Christians through our witnessing, and then we will be able to share this number with our friends or our church and gain status as church planters? Surely not! We know that the most important thing about sharing our faith in God is to help others experience the joy and encouragement we know through living prayer with God. God loves us and wants the best for us and for all persons.

Conversing with God in a life of prayer will lead us to find a joy that supersedes any circumstances. While the idea that something performed for three weeks will become a habit has been clearly debunked ("Habit Formation: The 21-Day Myth," *Forbes*,

Apr 15, 2013), nothing becomes a habit without being started and then continued. So, let's keep conversing with God as a way of living. And let's share this with others by how we live and how we talk about God and other persons. We want to love God as a response to God's love for us and then to love others in sacrificial caring for them that is triggered by God's love for us and others.

Living prayer means that we risk being open in continuous relationship with God about our deepest fears, desires, and joys and that we learn to trust our lives into God's hands regardless of the outcome of our conversations. Living in conversation with God is not so much asking for divine interference for us as it is developing a close, trusting, honest, and open relationship with God.

## TO DO:

I hope this time you have spent in studying about living prayer—both its scriptural basis and some practical aspects—has convinced you to keep trying to stay in close relationship with God's Spirit who lives in us and we live in the Spirit. I will keep praying and thanking God for you who have been readers of this book. I will try to answer all emails that come my way from readers. May God continue to walk with you and me and with those who will trust in God through our sharing of the good news of God through Christ Jesus. Amen!

Richard L. Bowman
richardbowman100@gmail.com
https://www.RichardLBowman.com

# Scriptural Index

www.ingramcontent.com/pod-product-compliance
Lightning Source LLC
Chambersburg PA
CBHW060401090426
42734CB00011B/2211